THE
HEART
OF KENDO

THE
HEART
OF KENDO

DARRELL MAX CRAIG

S H A M B H A L A
Boston & London
1999

Shambhala Publications, Inc.
Horticultural Hall
300 Massachusetts Avenue
Boston, MA 02115
www.shambhala.com

9 8 7 6 5 4 3 2 1

Designed by Dede Cummings Designs
First Edition
Printed in the United States of America
♾ This edition is printed on acid-free paper that meets the
American National Standards Institute Z39.48 Standard.

Distributed in the United States by Random House, Inc., and in Canada
by Random House of Canada Ltd.

Library of Congress Cataloging-in-Publication Data
Craig, Darrell.
    The heart of kendo/Darrell Max Craig—1st ed.
        p. cm.
    ISBN 1-57062-407-0 (alk. paper)
    1. Kendo.   I. Title.
    GV1142.C73   1999
    796.86—dc21   98-40527
                                                       CIP

CONTENTS

PREFACE

THIS book explains the origins, equipment, *waza* (techniques), and *kata* (exercises) of kendo, the Japanese way of the sword, as well as the traditions and the lifestyle or worldview one must adopt to follow its teachings. The book also presents biographical material about a man who is closely associated with this art: Harutane Chiba Sensei, thirty-seventh-generation scion of the Hokushin Itto Ryu Chiba family, a teacher who heavily influenced and altered my life. It would be almost impossible for me to convey accurately the depth of respect and reverence I have for kendo and its traditions without saying something about the personal experiences I have had as I followed its path.

The All Japan Kendo Federation has recently published a splendid Japanese-English dictionary of kendo, which defines *kendo* as "a form of *budo* which aims to train the mind and body and to cultivate one's character through one-on-one striking practice using the *shinai* [bamboo sword] while wearing *kendo-gu* [protective equipment]." Even closer to my own way of thinking about kendo is the following description, which appears at the beginning of the dictionary under the heading "The Concepts of Kendo": "Kendo is a way to discipline the human character through the application of the principles of the *katana* [long sword]." Thus kendo involves far more than studying the mechanics of striking with the sword. It involves a philosophy of life and an ethic of behavior. Mere drawings and step-by-step descriptions can never convey this essential dimension of kendo. However, careful attention to the words of a master can. For this reason I have included in this book—as verbatim as my memory would permit—many of the conversations I had over the years with my master, Chiba Sensei.

After studying many types of martial arts, I have come to several conclusions. First, at their core, all the martial arts, referred to collectively as *budo*, are the same. Moreover, if taught correctly, they are limitless journeys with no final destination. They are a way of life. The word *budo* has two elements: *bu*, or "martial," and *do*, which means "road," "lane," or "trail." *Budo* implies walking with pride, correct posture, and a purposeful stride, never deviating from the path. If you practice in this way, your *sensei*, or teacher, will do anything to guide you correctly. If you falter or become unwilling to make the necessary sacrifices, your *sensei's* guiding light will quickly extinguish. Once you step on this road, you begin an endless journey into the past, into a rich history and tradition. Without proper guidance, you will become lost. If, however, you secure a proper guide and follow him correctly, he will travel the road with you until death.

I have met and trained with some of the most knowledgeable martial arts teachers Japan has to offer. With their untiring guidance, I succeeded in discovering a few footholds on this endless path, sometimes being pulled, at other times pushed. The most frightening time was when, following my teacher, I literally entered into a cave. Suddenly, he blew out the light he was holding.

"Sensei," I said in a low voice.

No answer.

"Sensei, I can't see anything."

No answer.

"I can't see my hand in front of my face. Sensei, where are you?"

No answer.

"Sensei, are you all right?"

No answer.

"Sensei, this is not funny!"

"It wasn't meant to be."

"Where are you?"

"Where do you want me to be?"

"To help me find where in the hell you are!"

"I know where I am, and don't use that tone of voice."

"I'm sorry."

"I know you are now, but what about later?"

"Sensei, I promise I'll pay more attention to your guidance."

"I will not always be here to show you the way. You must pay attention at all times. To be given the light of knowledge so others can follow more easily is a great gift."

He relit the light and handed it to me, and as I took a firm grip, he vanished.

❖

It is impossible to master any art from a book. Neither text, drawings, nor photographs alone can show the rhythm and flow of the *waza*. Conversely, there is no limit to what one can learn from a good *sensei*, who is able to demonstrate the timing, posture, *maai* (proper distance), and coordination it takes to master the smallest kendo movement. Nevertheless, I hope this book will serve as a guide to the details and principles of kendo. I also hope it will be helpful to those small kendo clubs where a qualified *sensei* can come only infrequently. It is my sincere hope that this book will generate more interest and pleasure in *kata*. When you understand kendo's principles I know you will enjoy the feelings of confidence and well-being it produces. With time and practice, you will be able to carry this spirit into your daily life.

❖

I would like to thank Claudia Smith for her typing and patience; Gary Grossman, my jujitsu and karate student, who as always has done a wonderful job editing these manuscripts; Alan Park and Jimenez Blanco for their wonderful drawings; and especially O Sensei, Harutane Chiba of the Hokushin Itto Ryu, who before he left me on the trail to find my own way was always there with an encouraging word and a helping hand. As long as Chiba City in Japan lives and kendo throughout the world thrives, or so long as one person picks up a book to learn of the samurai families of Japan, Chiba Sensei's spirit will always be there.

Osaki Shigeharu Sensei, one of the foremost swordsmiths in Japan, looking for perfection in his art.

THE
HEART
OF KENDO

1
THE BEGINNING

THE year was 1966. I had been teaching karate for about a year when I received a telephone call from a Japanese gentleman. He was difficult to understand but kept asking me something like, "Do you do kendo?"

"Not only do I not do it," I explained to him, "but I don't even know what you are talking about. We do karate here."

He kept saying, "No, no. I do kendo." Eventually he said, "Never mind, never mind. No understand. I am coming to dojo. Please wait. Thank you. Good-bye."

About forty-five minutes later, the man who was to become my first kendo instructor, Jurato Yajima Sensei, arrived. He brought with him twenty *shinai* (bamboo swords) and two sets of *bogu* (armor). When I told him there was no one at the school with whom he could practice, he said something like, "Is okay, I teach, I teach." It dawned on me that he intended to teach me. I don't think he ever asked me if I wanted to learn kendo; he just informed me that he was going to instruct me. This encounter was the beginning of a path that I have followed ever since.

Yajima Sensei wasn't a tall man; by Japanese standards, twenty-odd years ago, he was of about average height. He didn't speak much English, so most of our lessons were taught by trial

Instruction from Jurato Yajima Sensei.

and error. I would try hard to follow his instruction, but the combination of the language barrier and my complete unfamiliarity with the art he was teaching made progress difficult. Sensei would explain the hip and foot work, then the correct way to make the cut. The harder I would try, the worse I would do. Sensei would say, "Hit my *kote* [glove]." But whenever I tried, it wasn't there, and his *shinai* would come crashing down on my head. Finally, after several months, I got the courage to ask Sensei, "How can I possibly hit your *kote* if you keep moving it?" He just smiled, took hold of my *men* (face protector), and twisted it so that I landed on my back. He quickly sat on the grille—which I was still wearing—grabbed the bottom of my *do* (chest armor), and proceeded to choke me unconscious with its top. I never asked many questions after that. He just led and I followed, which is really the best way.

Although the lessons were difficult, I discovered that I had a real love for kendo. My efforts were rewarded, and by 1968 I had received my *shodan*, or first-degree black belt. I had been practicing kendo for about five years when, in 1971, Sensei informed me, to my great excitement, that I was to participate in a kendo tournament in California. Unfortunately, my first experience at a *shiai* (contest) was something I would prefer to forget. Making mistakes is an integral part of the learning process, but it's painful nonetheless. Being the only Caucasian in the tournament, I was already off my guard, but my embarrassment reached its height when I foot-swept my first opponent, grabbed his *men*, and sat on it. I was about to start the choking procedure when the referees grabbed me under each arm and dragged me off the floor screaming something in Japanese I probably still don't want translated. Shortly thereafter, we were visited by a delegation from California informing Sensei that what he was teaching was pre–World War II kendo that was no longer acceptable in modern *shiai*. I received this news happily. My days of hip throws, foot sweeps, and head twisting—at least in kendo—came virtually to a close.

In retrospect, 1973 was a watershed year in my martial arts career, one in which several pivotal events happened to me. First, at the Second World Kendo Championships in Los Angeles and San Francisco, I met Setsuji Kobayashi Sensei, from the main department of the Imperial Palace Police. We talked, and shortly thereafter I was on my way to Japan again, this time by his invitation. The trip opened my eyes to a new world. Though Kobayashi Sensei's business card said Imperial Palace, I had no idea that I was actually going to practice kendo at the Imperial Dojo. Doing so is comparable to going to the White House and practicing self-defense with the Secret Service. Even though I had been practicing kendo for seven years when I first met him,

Shihan Kobayashi Sensei performing Hokushin Itto Ryu kenjitsu kata at the dojo of Harutane Chiba in Osaka, Japan, 1979. My son, Darren Craig, and a Houston student are in the background.

it was only through my experiences with Kobayashi Sensei that I really began to perceive the true art of kendo. My relationship with Kobayashi Sensei has lasted more than two decades and has been priceless to me. When I'm in Japan, Sensei always makes time for a lesson; his instruction has never grown dim.

However, the best was yet to come.

The aim of kendo, and of all Japanese martial arts, is not the perfection of a physical technique but the development of a flowing, flexible mind—a mind that is able to react to anything it confronts, instinctively, fearlessly, and without hesitation, regardless of the situation. Kendo is broken down into three parts: *kihon* (basics), *keiko* (practice), and *kata* (forms). Although this book touches on all three components, it deals most extensively with the last. But before delving into the specifics of *kata*, the balance of this opening chapter discusses some of the underlying principles that govern the art of kendo.

Harutane Chiba Sensei had a parable about water as it relates to training. "When you practice *kata* or *shiai*, the mind should always be the same: calm as a pond of water. Still water is like a mirror; it gives a picture of everything that is around it. But when the pond is disturbed, it reflects only the turmoil within its depths. You should always approach *shiai* and *kata* with a composure like the reflection on water in a pond, so the mind is relaxed, ready to see the slightest movement of your opponent."

Only by first understanding what *kendo kata* really is can you hope to use properly the skills (*waza*) that *kata* offers. Those skills include timing, balance, posture, speed, coordination, and self-discipline. Let's take just one of those six elements: posture, or in Japanese, *shizen hontai*. Whatever *kata* you perform, the posture you take during the action is critical to its success. Chiba Sensei once commented, "In the family scrolls of the Hokushin Itto Ryu it is written that when you have learned a *kata* properly it is as if you had not learned it at all. The movements of the *kata* will become as your everyday movements, showing no opportunity for an enemy to deliver his sword cut. A retainer [a samurai or warrior] of the family should study the *kata* until his posture at normal times is the same as at violent times." Proper posture must become instinctive. Until it does, you will not be able to execute a technique properly.

A highly developed posture allows the physical and mental balance necessary for the perfect *waza*. Chiba Sensei said that to understand kendo properly you must coordinate your mental spirit with your physical body. The smallest movement in kendo requires this coordination of body and mind. The body has no feeling without the five senses of the mind, yet the mind cannot exist without the presence of the physical body. If you do not coordinate these two elements, it would be like one hand trying to clap. Only when you bring both palms together will you produce the sound you seek. Only when you learn, through constant practice, to coordinate the body and the mind will you be able to realize their true function.

The Japanese say it should take you a lifetime to learn one *kata* perfectly.

When you practice *kendo kata* you must prepare your partner; that is, you must wait under his cutting sword until the very last second before you move. You must maintain your posture while the attacker thinks he has delivered a successful cut and until he realizes he has missed. This will allow him to make his cut naturally and then, at the last second, cause him to lose his balance both physically and—even more importantly— mentally. He will then pause to recover. His pause may be so brief that, unless your coordination is at its peak, you may find it impossible to take advantage of his bewilderment; your window of opportunity will close as quickly as it appeared. In *kendo kata* the *uchidachi* (teacher) usually moves first, followed by the *shidachi* (student). This allows the defender to match his movements with his opponent's. Only when you're skillful enough to match the opponent's movements can you seize the chance to apply your own *waza*. In other words, you must lead your *uchidachi* into such a position both mental and physical that the application of your own technique becomes quite easy. If your timing and balance is not in rhythm with the *uchidachi*, you will not be successful and may become off-balance yourself. This will allow the *uchidachi* to recover his equilibrium and open an excellent opportunity for him to counterattack. In a real duel, he most certainly would take advantage of this opportunity.

You must move your body against the *uchidachi* in a natural fashion, keeping a clear mind and allowing your spirit to flow outward. If the *uchidachi* disturbs your balance or posture, you probably will lose your spirit and he will easily defeat you. Chiba Sensei once said: "As the *uchidachi* makes his cut [in *kata*], your first thought as a beginner is to become stiff and rigid, to meet force with force, but as you master the sword through constant practice and find the proper understanding of its principles, you will receive the experience to meet your opponent without these tensions. You will find through continuous training the *waza* of *debana*, which depends upon a state called *sen*, in which you forestall your attacker by knowing the exact second he is going to cut and beginning your own *waza* against him immediately before his attack. To achieve *debana-waza* you must first control the attacker's mind before defeating his body."

My first question to Sensei as he was explaining *sen* was: "If you have the proper posture and spirit, where do you look?"

His answer was quite simple. "Be like the water in the pond. Take in everything. Be careful not to focus on any one thing. If you set your eyes on one place this will automatically set your mind on the same object. This will neglect other movements and you will become vulnerable to an attack."

"But Sensei, I thought you always said the eyes are the window to the mind."

"That is correct, but while looking at the eyes, see the *uchi-dachi* from side to side and top to bottom. Only with constant practice will you be able to sharpen your senses and develop these instincts of awareness."

In kendo, and especially in *kendo kata*, you must empty your mind of all preconceived ideas in order to see what is really there. You must be able to step from your mortal body into your spiritual mind; to move the mind into nonresistance. When one finds this path up the mountain trail it is like going from walking to riding. The trail doesn't become easier; you just don't tire as quickly. You'll find a feeling of tranquillity, of being at one with the sword and the spirit. This tranquillity will control the mind, and the mind will allow the body to move in a way only the masters know.

Most of us who study some type of combative discipline refer to what we do as a martial art. But strictly speaking, that term describes only those disciplines—the *bujutsu*, whose name literally translates as "martial arts"—that existed during the samurai era, which officially ended with the Meiji Restoration of 1868. Everything that came after that era, such as aikido, judo, and kendo, are *budo*—literally, "martial *ways.*" The Japanese ways of *budo* differ from the older martial arts of the samurai. Only gradually did the *-do* suffix replace the *-jutsu* or *-jitsu* suffix. For instance, as late as the 1930s Dr. Jigaro Kano's judo was still called jujitsu.

A samurai by the name of Chuta Nakanishi developed kendo's *bogu* (body armor) and *shinai* (bamboo sword) in the 1700s. Even before this—in 1668 or thereabouts—the word *kendo* was used. Master Gorodaiyu Abe, founder of the Abe Ryu, used the word *kendo* in his style of *kenjitsu*, which didn't differ in practice or theory from any other sword fighting of that era. The unification of Japan around 1600 ushered in an era of peace, and with it a fundamental change in the traditional *bujutsu*, which hitherto had been far too narrow in scope, adaptable only in times of war. One of Japan's most colorful samurai of the seventeenth century, Bokuden Tsukahara, traveled from one end of Japan to the other trying to seek out a deeper understanding of his kendo, convinced that there had to be a more noble or spiritual purpose to the *bujutsu*. Bokuden once told a fellow samurai that the ultimate use of swords was really in "killing one's own ego. Killing the opponent has become less important." Around the same time, Sakemochi Tsuji Sensei, founder of the Mugai Ryu, said similarly, "The art of swordsmanship, while teaching us to overcome an opponent, holds value for everyday life."

Chiba Sensei informed me that, according to dojo records that go back over 750 years, it wasn't until around 1860 that the Hokushin Itto Ryu started using the new body armor and the mock sword, even though many fencing halls had already adopted them. The change away from traditional *kenjitsu*, the old way of training in the dojo, came slowly. In traditional *kenjitsu* a student was taught exclusively by *kata*, using either the real *katana* (long sword) or a *bokuto* (wooden sword), which was just as dangerous.

After Harutane Chiba Sensei died, his katana was given to me by Frank Goishi Sensei, the head of the Chiba Dojo in Fresno. Sensei had left the wooden bokuto with me after his last trip to Texas, in 1991.

I asked Chiba Sensei about the significance of the word *Itto* in the name Hokushin Itto Ryu.

"*Itto* means 'one-sword style.'"

"Yes, I know that—but what does it mean?"

"To use one sword."

"Yes, Sensei, but were all sword styles Itto Ryu?"

"No."

"Other than Myamoto Musashi's two-sword style were there—"

"Oh! I see what you mean. Some people referred to a swordsman who had mastered the art of killing his opponent with one single stroke as an Itto stylist of *kenjitsu*. Of course, in those days if you couldn't kill your opponent with one stroke, you wouldn't have lived very long."

"Sensei, when do you think the biggest change came in *kenjitsu*?"

"In the Meiji era [1868–1912]."

"Why?"

"Probably because in 1874 or so the Meiji emperor abolished the practice of wearing swords."

"You mean there were no more samurai?"

"You could say that, but most important, the Meiji government was quite progressive minded. Emperor Mitsuhito insisted on Western attitudes and customs."

"So what did the samurai do?"

"I remember my father talking about those times, and from what I can remember, it must have been a bitter reality for the warring classes. The abolition of feudalism meant that the rifle would replace the sword; the common infantryman from peasant stock would be the new Japanese warrior. The samurai were forbidden the traditional hairstyle. It became against the law to wear swords in public."

"Did the samurai just give in?"

"Give in? What does that mean?"

"Give up, just accept what the government wanted."

"Oh. Some did, but many, like my family, became violently angry with the new laws. There were a series of attempted uprising and revolts."

"Did it do any good? Did anything change back?"

"No. All the conflicts were put down. But I know the samurai's resistance to the new government's ideas were fierce and long burning. There are still around today some people, like myself, who remember seeing old samurai and their children on the streets, topknot intact, defying the efforts of the police to enforce the haircutting law."

"So, Sensei, what happened to all the martial arts schools?"

"Some *sensei* stayed devoted to the old ways and eventually were lost in the dust of time. Fortunately for the future of Japan's martial arts, not all Meiji *sensei* were so set in their outlook to the future. My father, seeing the void left by the disappearance of the old *bujutsu*, slowly started teaching the spiritual aspects of the art through *budo*. The new way would allow the kendoists to retain their values of dedicated practice and self-perfection. This would allow the kendoists to restructure their goals to include positive ideas and benefit the Meiji government."

"Yes, Sensei, but did it change the way a student trained with a sword?"

"Now, that is a good question, not an easy one to answer."

"Why is that?"

"There were a lot of new dojos teaching only with *bogu* and *shinai* that were open to anyone who could pay the dues. On the other hand, dojos like ours were basically closed to the public. Entry was by invitation or a letter of introduction from someone my father knew. The rules for admittance were very strict. The lessons were twice daily, morning and evening. My father taught the morning classes most of the time, and they were almost always *kata* with a partner or solo. We used either a real sword or a wooden substitute. *Kata* would be performed with the feeling of a real duel, and the weapon would stop just before contact was made or blocked. I remember quite well being on the receiving end of many an accidental hit with the wooden *bokuto*. My father believed in teaching a *waza* only three times. He would start with one full week of explaining how the *waza* was applied. Then he would give you three weeks to practice it, either in *kata* or *uchikomi* [striking practice]. Then you faced him to see if you understood what you had been practicing."

"What happened, Sensei, if you didn't understand how it worked?"

"Oh, that's when you would be on the receiving end of an accidental hit on the head. My mother told me once I lay on the dojo floor for a day and a half."

"Why, Sensei?"

"My father told my mother that I was thinking."

"Thinking about what?"

"Father said that I needed time to think about what I was doing wrong."

"But Sensei, you might have died."

"Father thought that if you died, then you weren't learning the *waza*, and he could start at step one with someone new who might be able to learn it. It's really quite simple, Darrell: you need to practice very hard."

"Well, Sensei, I don't think the training from *bujutsu* to *budo* has changed all that much."

"No, not really until after World War II, when I reopened the dojo in 1951. We still do all the old *kata*, but not with the severe intensity of the Meiji era. Kendo is now taught not only for *waza*, as in classical *kenjitsu*. It now centers on three important principles: physical fitness (*rentaiho*), the fostering of education and morality (*shushinho*), and how to apply a technique (*shubuho*). A lot of Western thinking seems to be that kendo has no self-defense value but is only a sport; we call this *kyogi* in Japanese. I feel that nothing could be further from the truth. It is the individual who makes his or her art what other people see it to be."

"Sensei, do you feel *bujutsu* is lost forever?"

"As a samurai of the pre-Tokugawa era, yes. When we talk of *bujutsu* today we must look into history books. Like the knights of Europe who are colorful and picturesque they have outlived their usefulness. I can practice the old *kata* with you, and we together can keep the flickering light of the past alive, but only for history, so the new generation can have a glimpse into the Chiba style of kendo. Even now in our *kata* speed and cutting are not as important as self-control and etiquette. From *-jutsu* to *-do* has been a complex road. It started in the Meiji era and continues to the present. Equating martial arts with martial ways is a misconception that I feel lies in the way a *waza* is taught, and for what purpose it is taught. When someone says, 'Let's play kendo,' I immediately think of martial ways. On the other hand, when that same person says, '*Ippon shobu*' [a one-cut duel using real swords], my mind tells my body this is martial arts. With *ippon shobu* I know my life is at stake. *Bogu* and *shinai* are no longer of importance: he has a sword, I have a sword. Training will be the only factor in the duel. The kendoist must always focus on self-perfection through his martial training with all its commitments of spiritual discipline and hard practice. This new *budo* must benefit society and, to do so, *budo* cannot be a part of the martial artist's life: it must be his life."

Several times in my life, the contrast between martial arts and martial ways have been very evident. One such time was in 1979 at the Texas Renaissance Festival. The festival organizer asked me to present a kendo demonstration, offering the use of an area where another group—not a kendo group—was also going to present a demonstration. On a sunny Saturday morning about six students and I loaded our *bogu* and arrived at the site. I strung all the *bogu* on a long pole, shouldered the pole, and proceeded to the front gate. There a gentleman approached us wearing a European knight's helmet and carrying a sword and shield. Our paths were on a collision course, so I moved my little band off to one side so we could pass. He immediately adjusted to stay on a collision course. At this point I looked straight at him, wished him good morning, and asked him if he knew where the demonstration area was. The conversation then unfolded as follows:

"Why dost thou look for this place, knave?"

"What?"

"Art thou looking for the king?"

"No, we're here to put on a kendo demonstration."

"Is that not armor thou carriest upon the pole?"

"Yes, it's kendo armor for the demonstration."

At this point I motioned to the students to put the pole down. Before we could do so the "knight" took off his glove

Harutane Chiba Sensei and I demonstrating kendo kata at the Texas Renaissance Festival in 1981.

and threw it at my feet. I said, "You dropped your glove, partner."

"If thou art a man of honor, thou wilt pick it up and do
battle with me."

"What?"

"Art thou a coward, or dost thou have dung in those
ears?"

"Wait a minute, partner, are you challenging me to a
fight?"

"What else, knave?"

"Well, I'll tell you what, old buddy, if you just have a little patience until I can change, I'll be glad to accommodate you."

At this point, I removed my *bogu* from the pole and found a
place to change. On my return I found the young knight swinging his long sword to and fro impatiently. One of my students
handed me my *shinai,* and I thought we were ready. However, the
knight proclaimed in a loud voice, "That weapon is not acceptable in the rules of knighthood."

"What do you want me to use?"

He looked around where the *bogu* lay on the ground and
pointed to a wooden *tsuburi,* a heavy dueling sword.

"Oh, you have to be kidding—"

But before I could finish the sentence he said, "Art thou
afraid, knave?"

"Not for me," I replied. I reached over and picked up a heavy
Chiba *tsuburi,* a *bokuto* with a blunt end.

About this time I noticed that my young knight didn't appear
to be wearing any armor, just a jacket made of small pieces of
leather stapled together. I walked up to him and, feeling the
jacket, asked, "Do you have some kind of protection under that
jacket?" He stepped back, laid his long sword on his shoulder,
and took hold of his shield.

"Don't be concerned about this knight, knave. Prepare yourself to be taught some manners." So I took my *bokuto* in both
hands and assumed the central *chudan-no-kamae* position.

The next part I remember as if it were yesterday. Facing the young knight, I thought, "Let's see, if I go for his head, I bet he'll raise that shield to protect himself. I'm sure of one thing: if he hits me with that wooden sword it's going to hurt like hell. So I'd better not wait for him to make the first move." Just about that time I saw him drop his shoulder as if to help push off the sword. I screamed "*Men!*" and raised my *bokuto* to the *jodan* position. He responded by raising his shield to protect his head. In that split second I brought my *bokuto* down, screaming "*Do!*," and hit his right side just above the hip with all the strength I could muster. The blood was rushing through my body like a thousand fires. He fell straight down to his knees. I rushed forward with my *bokuto* over my head and started to deliver a blow to the top of his helmet. He dropped his sword and shield and raised his right palm toward me. "I yield," he said.

"Yield? What the hell does that mean?"

"I give up, sir knight. I quit."

"Oh, I see. Now that you've lost, I'm a knight. Before I was . . . what did you call it, a knave?"

At this point we moved off to find the place for our demonstration.

Looking back at this encounter years later, I must admit I don't take much pride in what happened. I let my ego take control of my body and common sense. The mind, once it becomes *senshin-teki-na*, as the Japanese say—once it escapes conscious control—then takes control of the body in turn. Although the body and mind have their own laws, the question is, Which should be the master, the body or the mind? To synchronize the spiritual mind and the physical body so that they are in tune is difficult. Yet if one cannot control them in *budo*, then one is not on the true path. I feel now that, although I won the fight, as a practitioner of kendo I lost the battle—with myself.

In January 1882, six years before he died, Yamaoka Tesshu

Sensei, who founded the No-Sword school of swordsmanship during the Meiji era, wrote:

> Those who correctly transmit the ultimate principles of swordsmanship have no special technique. They attain victory by entering their adversary's favorite place. What is the enemy's "favorite place" [i.e., his point of greatest strength]? Whenever two swords cross, all thoughts turn toward striking the opponent. By blending one's entire body with that of the opponent, one enters the opponent's favorite place and thus attains "victory through true victory." For example, prior to taking something from a box, one first removes the lid, looks carefully at the contents, and ascertains what it is. This is natural victory, requiring no special technique. However, even this procedure can become either extremely easy or extremely difficult depending on the approach. Students of the Way should not look at things in such simplistic terms.
>
> Swordsmen of other schools do not act in a natural manner. When they confront an opponent, they immediately get agitated and attempt to defeat the other swordsman through a hot-blooded frontal attack. This is a grave mistake. Those who practice in this way may be victorious in their youth when they are full of vigor and strength. However, when they no longer can depend on physical power due to age or ill health, their inadequately formed techniques will fail them—it is as if they had not studied swordsmanship at all, a needless waste of effort. This is false swordsmanship. Students of the Way must awaken to this principle while training harder and harder.*

Master Yamaoka Tesshu's thoughts on swordsmanship furnish us another insight into what the samurai was feeling as the country changed slowly from *bujutsu* to *budo*. The mental training of Master Tesshu, which, aligned with technical ability,

*Quoted in John Stevens, *The Sword of No-Sword* (Boston: Shambhala Publications, 1984), p. 128.

Hakudo Nakayama Sensei (right) and Sasaburo Takano Sensei (left) performing kodachi ipponme, the first kendo technique using the short sword, at a special kata demonstration for the imperial household around the turn of the century. In Japan one cannot speak of modern kendo without acknowledging Hakudo Nakayama Sensei, an outstanding kendoist. His large handlebar mustache, combined with his knowledge of the sword, made him awe-inspiring to behold. Probably more books and articles have been written about him and his thoughts about swordsmanship than about any other kendoist of that era.

physical health, and educational fitness, prevailed in the martial arts scene in Meiji Japan, is what martial arts should be today but so often is not. Although it is challenging to meet an opponent in competition and to defeat him, that is only a small part of kendo. The real goal is to win over yourself, to discipline and train your mind.

The traditional aspects of *budo* and *bujutsu* in Japanese culture have a certain appeal to people of other countries who seem to thrive on severe discipline. The *sensei* of a dojo will almost always make a new student—regardless of rank—practice the most basic techniques for up to hours at a stretch. If the student perseveres, his feet and palms will become raw and bleed. As the days and months go by, he will see new students arrive at the dojo, only to depart, unwilling to undergo the iron discipline the *sensei* demands. I have seen many foreign and Japanese enthusiasts give up when they are confronted with the hard feudalistic training that a traditional dojo—such as Chiba Sensei's—requires.

The students who are truly dedicated to mastering Japanese *budo* will slowly move forward and acquire the advanced black belt ranks, even become teachers in their own right. All of this brings us back to the question, What is the difference between *bujutsu* and *budo*? If you were to ask a practitioner who has gone through this feudalistic training the answer would be: very little. If you asked the same question of someone who hasn't had this type of training, he would probably reply that the modern -*do* forms, unlike their -*jutsu* counterparts, place an emphasis on sporting competition. This is where the misunderstanding about *kendo kata* arises.

The emphasis on sport kendo has stunted the growth of *kata* for the average kendoist. *Kata* is vital not only to the individual kendoist but to the art as a system. *Kata* must be emphasized as a training method and not just used for demonstration. The true essence of *kata* is not often placed before the average student, who thus sees *kata* as something weak, almost useless. Today, the general perception of *kata* is so distorted that more than one kendo master has expressed doubt whether the true meaning of *kendo kata* will survive another generation. In America, much of the blame lies with kendo instructors themselves. If you were to ask seven teachers, "What is the importance of *kata*?" you would probably get at least five different answers. If you asked each one a question about one part of a specific *kata*, the differences in their responses would probably be even greater.

I was once asked to help teach a *kendo kata* clinic in the

United States with three well-known instructors. As I began to teach the small group assigned to me, I was immediately stopped. "What are you teaching?" a *sensei* asked.

"The basics of *ipponme* [the first kendo *kata*]."

"Well, that is all wrong."

"This is the way Sensei ———— from Japan showed me last year."

"Well, that was last year. Now we are doing it a new way. You must have the videotape the All Japan Kendo Federation has been sending out."

"Yes I do, and that is the way I thought the Japanese Federation wanted it taught."

"That may be the way they want it taught, but it's not the way we want it taught here."

If you think this was confusing to me, how do you think the students felt? Many kendoists complain that the *kata* they are being taught is subject to the instructor's interpretation. How can a student learn *kata* when one *sensei* says one thing and another says something else? *Kendo kata* as it is taught by the governing bodies, the All Japan Kendo Federation and International Kendo Federation, is standardized. At any time, there is only one technically correct way. (One must remember that there are literally thousands of old sword *kata* in existence in Japan; the two governing bodies determine the *standardized* form.) Over the years, this standard *kendo kata* has been modified many times, and teachers who have not kept up to date may be using obsolete concepts. Some employ their own personalized versions of *kata*; these are usually the product of their lack of knowledge. Here again, to seek out the truth about *kendo kata*, the student must select a qualified instructor.

An interesting thing about *kata* is that—when practiced or demonstrated with real swords—it is the only time that the kendoist faces death with each move. Also, when *kata* is performed correctly it teaches coordination of the body and mind. Chiba Sensei called it *ki-ken-tai-ichi*, or "spirit, sword, and body

The author holding a katana.

are one." *Kata* teaches the three most important things you need in *shiai*. The first is *sensen-no-sen*; this is a *waza* in which both opponents plan to attack but one is quicker and strikes first. The second is *go-no-sen*; here one opponent attacks and the other parries and then applies his own *waza*. Finally, there is *sen-zen-no-sen*, where one opponent attacks and the other dodges the attack and then counterattacks.

In *kata* the sword becomes an extension of one's spirit. It becomes, as the old samurai say, one's "very soul." The body is the only link between the two. Only when you use a real sword and experience the fear of death—or at least the thought that you might get cut—can kendo come alive in each *kata*. This feeling forces the spirit, mind, and sword to function as a single unit. When practiced on a regular basis, *kata* eliminates doubt and fear within the practitioner and develops a truly proficient swordsman.

Kata has become nothing more to some kendoists than something they have to learn just before a rank exam. Once they receive their *menjo* (certificate), they forget it. Without *kata*, kendo is lopsided and furnishes little recognition of the traditional values. In Japan, kendo is now widely taught with competition constantly in mind. This attitude of practicing only to win is a big mistake. Kendo should be practiced for its own sake, not for the sole purpose of winning a match. Here in the United States, students enter kendo tournaments with only a few months of instruction, completely ignorant of the philosophy and traditions of the art, such as discipline, manners, and obligation. One who practices kendo should not look for rank or power and should refrain from bringing violence into his or her training. In some respects kendo has changed so much in the last few decades that it would probably be unrecognizable to its Meiji-era founders.

Kata, which has been an integral part of kendo for centuries, has two distinctive developmental stages. Stage one, the "doing" stage, involves practicing and studying the mechanical aspects of the *kata*. This is the time when the student concerns himself with every technical aspect and the smallest detail of the *kata*. Although this first stage has little value as a complete training tool, once one understands the basic principles of the *kata* and can perform them to some degree of proficiency, one can then proceed to the second, or "using," stage. Although *kata* can be begun at any level of training, it is perhaps best started at the third novice class, or *sankyu* level (see chapter 7). According to the All Japan Kendo Federation rules for promotions, *kata* is not begun until *ikkyu*, or first-degree brown belt.

The dojo does not exist solely for the purpose of mastering the sword but also to hand down knowledge. True knowledge of kendo, like skill, cannot be taught; it can be acquired only through long hours of practice and training. Generally, knowledge is a process of self-discovery that occurs—if at all—only after a qualified teacher has put the student on the correct path. Skill, on the other hand, is linked with wisdom and the capacity for learning and self-discipline. The *hombu*, or "home" dojo gives the satellite dojos, called ryuha, the perceptions, experiences, and accumulated knowledge along with the common sense collected over centuries by past masters of the *ryu*; this avoids the *ryuha* from having to begin the discovery process from scratch. This skill and knowledge is handed down in the *ryu*'s *kata*. If practiced correctly, the traditional *kata* becomes a ritualized combat, an exercise in aesthetic movement. It establishes the *ryu*'s fundamentals; it is a type of moving meditation. It allows the student to build self-confidence while facing an opponent with a real sword.

One of the most essential features of *kata* is the lesson it teaches: namely, that if one truly understands the principle of the *kata*, the principle and the *waza* are undivided, like a person and his shadow. However, the teacher or the student should always emphasize the polishing of the *waza* itself. It will become evident that, with training, the principle will manifest itself spontaneously.

The *sensei* of a *ryu* transfers the *waza* and the *kata* to the student; in doing so, he illuminates that *ryu's* principles. The *sensei* presents the rules of action or conduct while creating an environment in which the student can understand and absorb them. The student must realize from the first day he steps into the *sensei's* world that all lessons are a gradual developmental process in which the sensei helps the student incorporate within himself the guiding principles of the *ryu's* doctrine. The mastery of each *kata* or *waza* must come from the student's own efforts. To illustrate this, consider a mother trying to teach her daughter to ride a bicycle. The child only knows she wants to ride. She does not understand the principles of pedaling or steering, let alone how to balance on two wheels. Most important, she is unlikely to discover how to do this by herself. At the same time, no one can fully explain these elements to her. The mother can only demonstrate them and help the child practice them. The *sensei* with a student who refuses to practice sufficiently is like the mother whose daughter refuses to try to ride. The mother usually gives the bicycle a push. The daughter is afraid to jump off. One of two things happen: either the child will crash and refuse to try again, or she will determine for herself which muscles are needed at what times to make riding the bicycle possible. The *sensei,* like the parent, must ultimately leave it to the student to decide what is important. Once the student decides to climb back on the bicycle, it is very important for the *sensei* to understand that the student seeks the knowledge, and to carefully guide him through the right kind of experience so he can achieve the right kind of understanding.

An old saying among the Japanese samurai goes: "For your friends you spill tears. For your country you spill blood. For your family you spill sweat." Only through sweat can you push back your ego and obtain severe discipline within yourself.

The new student must master the *ryuha's kata* by copying them; that is, by learning and absorbing the principles and secrets inherent in the master's techniques, without altering them in any way. He should not try to analyze them, either. When I first started learning *kata*, I had a thousand questions, all of which seemed important at the time. Now I can't remember even one. It's not that I have mastered the *kata*; rather, the answers have emerged from the *kata* one by one and, in any event, are not as important as mastering the basic moves the *kata* offers. I have learned that one must struggle to learn, and that defeat never comes from without. It is not the sword's fault if the cut is untrue. While teaching me a movement in a *kata* one day, Sensei said, "Always remember, nothing is ever repeated. Each *kata* movement is different. Even if you repeat it one thousand times, it is different each time. The similarity is only in the mind. Learning to master the smallest part of a *kata* is not a commodity. You cannot buy it at the store. It is obtained only with the individual's effort, and it will come in its own fashion and time."

At one time in Japanese history a samurai could test his *kata* skills, or the free-flowing *waza* the *kata* has to offer, in what was called *musha-shugyo* or *dojo-yaburi* (also known as *dojo-arashi*), two forms of "dojo storming." This was done by traveling about the country seeking instruction and engaging in duels or sparring matches. *Musha-shugyo* refers to the circumstance whereby a samurai had permission to leave his own dojo with a letter of introduction from the master of his school. He would travel to the mountains and practice his *kata* through *uchikomi* and meditation. When he felt he was ready he would then travel to a city where he had heard of a strong kendo dojo or where his *sensei* knew the fencing master. He then presented his letter of introduction and requested a kendo match. Usually the master of the dojo would send out his strongest student first to meet the challenge. If the *musha-shugyo* samurai defeated this student, the master might not pick up the challenge himself, instead making some excuse and usually giving the samurai some money for traveling expenses and sending him on his way—in those days, if the master were beaten, it would be the end of that school. On the other hand, if the *musha-shugyo* samurai were beaten, he would stay and become a devoted pupil until he felt he had mastered that dojo's *waza* and then move on.

Dojo-yaburi, whose name translates as "school storming," was something entirely different. It was never looked upon as a friendly challenge and was not accepted in a light manner. The samurai who engaged in this type of traveling and challenging usually was an experienced swordsman with only one or two things in mind. One, he would make the challenge knowing that the dojo did not have a strong student fencer and that the fencing master was old and trying to make a living on his past reputation. In this case an instructor would offer him a large sum of money with an apology that there was not anyone of his quality at the dojo. This was frequently what he was after to begin with, so he would take the money and depart. On the other hand, he might be after something else, in which case he would act insulted by the offer and kill one or two of the dojo's instructors, thus sending a message back to the fencing master that he wanted a kendo match. The master then knew that the samurai was after a more famous reputation and that the very heart of the dojo was at stake. When this happened the dojo students would frequently try to ambush the samurai and kill him. If this didn't succeed, the dojo was usually lost; the samurai usually killed the dojo's master and as many of his students as he could, then moved on with his new reputation to meet new challenges.

Chiba Sensei once told me a story about one of his ancestors, Shusaku Chiba (1793–1855), who had left his home on a *musha-shugyo* pilgrimage. He traveled to Edo in 1809 with a letter of introduction to Matashichiro Takai Sensei, who had a following of thousands of students, and became his pupil in the Itto Ryu style. After a short time with the dojo, Takai Sensei was so impressed with Shusaku Chiba that he decided to ask for a personal duel with the young samurai, something that in those days was almost unheard of. The teacher had everything to lose and little to gain. The pupil, on the other hand, had absolutely nothing to lose, and if by some chance he were victorious, he would become instantly famous.

The duel took place at the dojo of a friend of Takai Sensei's in Edo named Chube Nakanishi. Nakanishi's dojo was one of the best-known dojos in Edo and was famous for its wooden floor, which was one and a quarter inches thick and made of red oak imported from China. It was set on willow wood, which gave it a kind of floating feeling, as if one were on water.

Shusaku Chiba knew that no one had ever beaten Takai Sensei in a duel. He also knew this would be a great opportunity to try out his own *waza*, on which he had been secretly working. The duel started, and after what seemed forever—mainly because no one could gain the advantage—Shusaku Chiba gave a tremendous *kiai*, or shout, which was followed immediately by a loud crack from the floor. With one *tsuki* (thrust) to the face he beat Takai Sensei—and gave such a mighty stomp as he did so that he broke through the floor as well. A couple of days later, the dojo owner cut out the broken flooring and had it framed and put on display so that all could see the tremendous power released by Shusaku Chiba's *tsuki*. Shortly after this encounter Shusaku Chiba set up his own dojo and had it officially recorded with the Japanese government as the Hokushin Chiba Itto Ryu. A woodblock print circulated around 1811 shows Shusaku Chiba breaking through the floor during the duel at Nakanishi's dojo.

During the nineteenth century the teaching of martial arts began to emerge throughout Japan as a profession. Highly skilled kendo teachers no longer needed to train young samurai for war because, under the Tokugawa rule, there were no wars to prepare for. Samurai such as Shusaku Chiba devoted themselves fully to instructing students for fees. This instruction was done with *kendo-gu* and through *kata*. For the traditional masters, *kata* became the heart of their *ryu*. The old *taryu-jiai,* or

Two-part woodblock print showing a kenjitsu match using bokuto (wooden swords) between the samurai Tokichiro Kino-shita (1537–98) on the left and the fencing master Kahei Matsushita on the right. A few years later, Tokichiro Kinoshita changed his name to Hideyoshi Toyotomi and became shogun of Japan.

contest between the two dojos using the *bokuto,* or wooden sword, became frowned upon by the *ryu* themselves. Moreover, the Japanese government stepped in and prohibited the *taryu-jiai* without special governmental permission, which wasn't given very often. By 1860 the Japanese government put an end to *taryu-jiai* altogether. With this government cap on *taryu-jiai,* the battlefield kendo masters started to disappear from the open scene because they could no longer prove their battle skills in open or public combat. This had one fortunate aspect for the kendo instructor who had never seen battle with a real sword; it afforded him an excuse to avoid such confrontations. These kendo instructors relied upon *kata* almost entirely. One result was that their students grew further and further away from the real dueling experience needed to understand why one moved this way or that in a *kata.* Such a swordsman was referred to as *kenpo-kaho,* or "one who plays at swordsmanship." Old kendo masters would make fun of them by saying things like "their *waza* is like *ikebana* [flower arrangements] without a vase. Beautiful to look at—but don't touch or it will fall apart."

Because old traditions such as *taryu-jiai* are hard to break, let alone control, the practice was not eliminated completely even though prohibited by the Japanese government. When Shusaku was about thirty years old, he and his Hokushin Itto Ryu were challenged to a *taryu-jiai* by Maniwa Nen Ryu, one of the leading kendo dojos in Japan. This was all brought about because Shusaku Chiba, in a duel, killed a Maniwa Nen Ryu student who was supposed to have been a real *shinken* warrior (i.e., a samurai who did not believe in *bogu* and used only a real sword in practice). The date was set and, by the time the *taryu-jiai* was to take place, hundred upon hundreds of kendo enthusiasts and students gathered outside the Maniwa Nen Ryu dojo. They all wanted to witness what was rumored to be the battle of the century. Shusaku Chiba appeared with about two hundred students of the Hokushin Itto Ryu and was faced with a similar number of Maniwa Nen Ryu samurai. According to the Chiba family hand scrolls, what took place next was almost unbelievable.

Because of the large numbers involved in the *taryu-jiai,* small fights broke out almost spontaneously. For unknown reason, the duels that were in progress when the town's chief magistrate showed up were with *bokuto*; real swords were still in their resting places. The chief magistrate had brought about one hundred police officers with him. Because he had his officers take down the names of everyone involved so he could report them to the officials in Edo, the fighting gradually settled down without a major riot. When the smoke had cleared there were fifty-three casualties on the Meniwa Nen Ryu side and only three on the Chiba side. Shusaku Chiba was considered the last of the old-style fencing masters who taught professionally.

In the year before Shusaku Chiba's death in 1855, Japan was practically torn apart by the arrival of the American fleet led by Commodore Perry. This eventually ended Japan's two centuries of self-imposed isolation and changed the way of the samurai forever.

questioned, but the application required the information. Looking as though he had seen something for the first time, he replied, "Samurai have no rank; only peasants have rank." I closed the subject, scribbled something respectable on the application, and mailed it.

I think our relationship could best be described as one of father to son. His instruction was always with a firm hand but an understanding heart. He never left a question unanswered or a technique unfinished. I was the clay and he was the master potter, molding and hardening me at his whim. In 1979 the Houston Budokan became the first branch office of the Hokushin Chiba Ryu outside of Japan. It wasn't until several years later that Sensei opened a second branch, this one in Fresno, California.

Another vignette involves our first deer hunting experience, in 1978. Few Japanese have any firearm experience, and I had taken O Sensei to the rifle range once to get him acquainted with the rifle he was to use. We then loaded up the truck and headed off to the hill country of West Texas, along with several of my students. I explained to Sensei that he was allowed to shoot one deer with antlers and one deer without. The morning of the hunt, my student Bill Smith and I took Sensei to his tree stand. After I again explained where to aim and confirmed that he understood the one buck and one doe limit, he gave us the high sign and we left. We were just settling down in our own stand when the sun peeked over the horizon. There was barely enough light to make out the shadowy objects when the sound of two rifle shots from Sensei's direction broke the silence. I remember looking at Bill and saying, "I hope he hasn't shot another hunter. It's too damn dark to see anything." We jumped in the truck and started up the hill only to be met by Sensei walking casually down the road puffing away on his pipe. As we rolled to a stop, Bill asked if he had shot twice. Sensei nodded yes. "Did you get anything?" Sensei held up two fingers. I looked at Bill, Bill looked at me, and we both began to snicker. Sensei climbed aboard and we returned to his stand. His rifle was leaning against a tree. We looked around

Frank Goishi Sensei, the head of Chiba Dojo in Fresno, California (right); Toshitane Chiba Sensei, now head of the Hokushin Chiba Dojos (center); and me, in Fresno, 1993.

and couldn't see anything. Then Sensei pointed in an easterly direction. We started walking and, at about the seventy-five-yard mark, there lay an eight-point buck perfectly shot. Bill and I started to get excited, and I said to Sensei, "This is a great shot and a nice rack. You're a pretty good hunter for the first time out, but it did take you two shots to get him." Sensei just walked another fifteen yards directly in line with the buck. We quickly followed, and there, to our wondering eyes, was a doe shot in almost exactly the same place.

We loaded up Sensei's trophies and headed back to the cabin. As Sensei watched, Bill and I set about with the cleaning and skinning. When I asked Sensei what he thought about deer hunting, he took a long puff on his pipe, let out the smoke, and said, "There's really not a lot to it, is there?" He pointed for us to remove the backstrap from the deer. Sensei cut it into very small round wafers and poured soy sauce over it, and we all sat down and ate breakfast—raw.

Chiba Sensei always enjoyed Texas. He felt that the spirit of the Old West and the spirit of the Japanese samurai were really the same. He saw a great similarity between the western cowboy with his two guns and the samurai with his two swords. The descendants of the true Texas cowboys, he felt, retained the cowboy spirit, just as he—a descendant of the original samurai—retained the samurai spirit. Sensei was also dedicated to seeing the spirit of kendo survive and believed that one way to achieve this was to expose more non-Japanese people to kendo. He believed that the teachings of the samurai had applicability even in the modern world, and that these teachings could be learned through the study of kendo. Sensei always thought that the spirit of kendo contributed significantly to Japan's high productivity. He said, "Through kendo you keep the mind in good shape and the spirit strong. Kendo develops good reflexes, and on Japanese streets we need it. Kendo consists of more than strong techniques. It builds a strong sense of justice, social duty, and respect for others. Kendo is a code of conduct, an art that teaches discipline, and an activity that provides exercise." Sensei once told me that, although kendo had long ago been dropped as a military defense technique, true swordsmen had retained its philosophical elements. "A samurai should never kill. It's like the United States having nuclear weapons. They don't want to use them but they wear them as a badge. The weapons give the countries enough confidence to keep the peace. A kendo man who kills another kills a part of himself and casts discredit on other kendo men."

In 1979 I made my first trip to Sensei's dojo in Osaka. It was on this trip that the honor of which I am the most proud was bestowed upon me and my son; we became the first non-Japanese to be inducted into the Chiba family. We had become samurai. After the presentation we were informed by other Japanese, who were not in the clan, that we were no longer ordinary swordsmen; now we were upholders of a great tradition, one that we had to guard with our very lives if need be. In the process we were awarded the *haori*, the traditional samurai coat. This surcoat, along with the traditional fan, are the badges of membership in the clan known as Chiba Hokushin Itto Ryu, a name that translates as "the one-sword style of the north star," referring to the style of fencing created by Tsutane Chiba (1118–1212), a member of the seventh generation of the Chiba family and an ancestor of Harutane Chiba Sensei.

The *haori* I received was handmade from raw silk by Sensei's family and has five crests embroidered on it. Traditionally it is to be worn for special events and formal occasions along with the kimono and *hakama*. Each clan has its own mark or coat of arms that distinguishes it from the other clans. An individual samurai could have his own family coat of arms, but once taken into a traditional clan and presented the fan and *haori*, he wore the *haori* over his own coat of arms. Only a man born into or adopted by a samurai family was allowed to wear this distinguishing badge and the *diasho*, or two swords. The badge, which in times past was about twelve inches in diameter, is now about one and a half inches in diameter. The Chiba mark consists of a large crescent shape, the ends of which almost meet to form a circle, near the top of which is a dot. The dot represents the north star and the crescent represents the universe; signifying that once a clan member has drawn his sword, he becomes the north star and never moves. Everything in the universe must go around him.

Harutane Chiba wasn't a man of great height, yet he seemed much taller than he really was. His conversations were concise; his words were like a final blow on a nail head. He made his point firmly and left you with substance on which to build. Sensei Chiba was one of the last of his kind. He walked with an air that set him apart from other men, yet he was the most humble man I ever knew. I knew him for fifteen years and I cannot recall his ever raising his voice. A mysterious aura seemed to surround him and his subjects when he instructed.

The following are samples of exchanges Chiba Sensei and I had over the years. I have reconstructed them from notes and memories to the best of my ability, aware that the mind can play tricks with what is heard and what is really said.

1978

CRAIG: Sensei, what does "Hokushin" mean?

SENSEI: The style of the north star.

CRAIG: Yes, I know that, but what is its real meaning?

SENSEI: A man who studies the Hokushin Ryu style of fencing should never vary from what he feels to be correct, whether he's in a fencing match or dealing with daily strife. A Hokushin family man will always stand behind the family's decisions, firmly and to the end. Thus, once the sword is drawn, like the north star he never moves and everything in the universe must revolve around him.

CRAIG: Sensei, who started the style of Hokushin?

SENSEI: That's very difficult to answer. The Chiba family is more than seven hundred and fifty years old, approximately thirty-eight generations. But if I were to give credit to one individual member of the family, it would probably be Shusaku Chiba, who was born in the 1700s and died in 1855.

CRAIG: I don't understand. Was the style called something else before 1700?

SENSEI: No. It just wasn't registered as an official style. In the mid-1700s it was officially registered with the Mito Bakufu as the Hokushin Itto Batto-tai Ryu. Hokushin Ryu became the official style of *kumitachi* [*kenjitsu*] for the Mito Han officials. It is my understanding that Shusaku Chiba Sensei had at this time a dojo in Edo [Tokyo] called Gembukan with more than five thousand students.

CRAIG: Sensei, that doesn't sound like a dojo. It sounds like an army.

SENSEI: Well, it was, in an unofficial way. The prime purpose of the Chiba family was to protect the welfare and officials of the emperor. The Chiba family had a following so large that it literally created its own city, which exists to this very day, known as Chiba City in the prefecture of Chiba. This encampment guarded the main entrance into and out of Edo. As some of you Westerners would say, there are many hidden stories in the big city.

CRAIG: I know, Sensei. That's what I'm trying to dig out. What do you think is the most important difference between the family at that time and the present?

SENSEI: My real feeling is that no one was allowed to ask so many questions.

CRAIG: I'm sorry, Sensei. I don't mean to be discourteous, it's just that I want to know more about Japan's history and you are the key to the door that I've found.

SENSEI: It's OK to ask questions. Things are so much different now from when I was a boy. The problem with questions is that sometimes you find something you weren't looking for and then you're unable to handle it. Questions should always be balanced with the proper amount of training. Training should always be balanced with the proper amount of discipline. It seems to me that we want things without the proper training or discipline to achieve them. This is where kendo becomes the heart of the student. The student should follow the teacher without question or put down his sword. The Japanese have a saying: "If you wear the badge, you carry the burden."

1979

CRAIG: Is *mokuso* [sitting meditation] important at the beginning and end of a lesson?

SENSEI: *Mokuso* is one of the most important disciplines in any *budo*. My father believed that a man is divided in two parts equally. The left side, being closer to the heart, is the good side, and the right side is the evil. Sitting in proper *seiza* [sitting position] and doing *mokuso* helps us in finding our true self—not what other people see us to be, and not what we think we are, but what we really are, good and evil. The left hand rests on top of the right hand. The thumbs form a circle just above the navel; the arms should be in a circular position. *Mokuso* is intended to increase the power of concentration by slowly eliminating all distractions from the mind. Most Westerners do not understand the full meaning and find it very difficult to concentrate on only one thing at any given moment.

CRAIG: I'm confused, Sensei. I'm trying to follow and desperately hang on to what you're saying.

SENSEI: See, I told you. It takes concentration. Close your eyes and try to blank out all thoughts from your mind just for a few moments. . . . It's very difficult to think of nothing even for a short time. Through constant practice of *mokuso* you will eventually discover your inner consciousness and experience the illumination of your own ego. In other words, you will see your complete self. Some people call this a state of total tranquillity—nirvana.

CRAIG: This is all good and true for you, Sensei, but as a beginner what should I be thinking of?

SENSEI: I just told you! But if you have to have an answer to satisfy your Western way, why don't you try to do away with your ego?

CRAIG: OK, Sensei. Let me ask you this, getting back to the good and bad sides. If I understand you correctly, the left hand, which is the good, is suppressing the naughty right hand.

SENSEI: Naughty hand? What's a naughty hand?

CRAIG: The bad hand.

SENSEI: Yes. The good should always hold back the bad.

CRAIG: Is that why the left hand always precedes the right hand when we bow?

SENSEI: Don't you feel that the good should always guide and help the weak and misguided?

CRAIG: When did you first start kendo?

SENSEI: My life as a child ended when I became of school age. This is when my life began to become highly disciplined. I was called before my father and the elders of the dojo and was told that I was no longer an infant and from this day forward I must act accordingly. From this day forward I had to respect the elders and *sensei* and discipline myself to be different from most children in the village. I was to practice in the dojo twice daily, morning and evening.

CRAIG: Did you find this difficult?

SENSEI: I don't think I ever thought about it one way or the other. Being born into a samurai family is your destiny, not your choice.

CRAIG: You know so much and I seem to know so little.

SENSEI: Knowledge is free for the taking. We are exactly the same but totally different in many ways. We are both climbing to the top of Myuoho Mountain. While I started before you, you're watching from below and wishing to be where I am. I have no time to keep looking back to see where you are, for it would slow down my own progress. We are both beginners, but each at a different level. I burn the candle at both ends, which makes it easier for you to find the proper footholds, but you must find each one by yourself. I, looking forward, also feel like a beginner and illuminate the way. Each bend in the path finds new and exciting things for each of us.

CRAIG: Will I ever be like you, Sensei?

SENSEI: Why would you want to be? You must be yourself. Never copy another man's dreams. I cannot teach you anything. I can only show you. It is up to you to discipline your life in such a way that you can teach yourself once you've been shown the correct direction. Do you understand what I'm saying?

CRAIG: I think so, but what will I do when you're no longer here to show me the correct path?

SENSEI: If you pay strict attention to the basics in kendo and never vary from their path, you will always be able to return to the beginning if you lose your way. It is my job to lead you around sharp turns and avoid dead ends. It is your job to make sure that with each step you have secured a proper foothold. Timing, balance, posture, and discipline are the elements to construct whatever is needed to reach your objective.

1980

CRAIG: Sensei, I'd like to ask a question.

SENSEI: I know.

CRAIG: I'm sorry.

SENSEI: I know. What is your question?

CRAIG: What is a koan?

SENSEI: It is a puzzle, sometimes referred to as a riddle, given by Zen masters to novice priests to solve.

CRAIG: Could you give me an example?

SENSEI: I could, but I'm not a Zen priest and you're not a
novice priest.

CRAIG: But, Sensei, I am a novice.

SENSEI: I think you're learning. OK. Suppose a farmer takes an
egg from a chicken and places it in a bottle. He places the
bottle in conditions favorable for hatching the egg. Instead of taking the chicken out of the bottle after it has
hatched, the farmer feeds it every day until it has matured.

CRAIG: Sensei, that's stupid.

SENSEI: Shut up. You asked a question. Now listen to the answer. If you were a good student, you wouldn't be asking
the question to begin with. Just kidding! The chicken has
matured. Now the farmer decides to sell the chicken, but
the chicken has grown too large to be removed from the
bottle. How was the farmer able to remove the chicken
from the bottle without breaking the bottle? You may not
ask any more questions until you give me the answer.

1981

CRAIG: Sensei, remember that stupid koan about the chicken
and the bottle?

SENSEI: Yes. Do you remember what I said about any more
questions?

CRAIG: Yes. But, Sensei, I don't know the answer. Can you give
me a little hint?

SENSEI: That's another question.

CRAIG: Sensei, I cheated. I bought a bunch of Zen books and I
have come to the conclusion that you tricked me.

SENSEI: That's Zen.

CRAIG: But Sensei, anyone who actually finds an answer to
your koan has failed. It is my understanding that koans
are given to ponder about the impossible day after day.
They're a kind of shock treatment to a person's mind to
help to open the gate to the intuitive mind. Koans are

given to help condition the mind so it's capable of accomplishing a higher degree of concentration.

SENSEI: Without knowing what you were asking, you have come up with someone else's solution. But we must learn from everybody. A novice priest would ponder over a koan given him for years. Even after concentrating on it endlessly he would have not found a solution to the riddle. Sooner or later the novice would notice that he is able to meditate for long periods of time before any other thoughts but the riddle could enter his mind. Eventually he would be able to meditate without a koan to solve. Meditation with a koan is referred to as concentration with seed, whereas meditation without any thought is just the opposite. I feel after our practice together today that in these months when we have been separated you have taken one more solid step forward. What do you think?

CRAIG: I can't see myself as others do.

SENSEI: I can't believe now you've got me asking the questions. But you are progressing forward.

CRAIG: What do you think is the most important part in kendo?

SENSEI: To cut down one's own ego. People today search for identity from all parts of the world around them when they should be searching within themselves.

CRAIG: What do you have to lose by not practicing on a daily basis?

SENSEI: Nothing but your life. You've already lost your discipline.

CRAIG: Where should you find yourself during kendo practice?

SENSEI: On the end of your sword. A man is measured by another man through the temper of the steel he carries outwardly and within himself. If his mind is straight, his cutting actions will be straight. His sword and body should move in unison with each other.

1982

CRAIG: Sensei, I have built a Japanese village about thirty miles north of Houston. Would you be agreeable to the idea of demonstrating kendo there one or two times on the weekend?

SENSEI: Do you need me to?

CRAIG: Well, Sensei, of course it would be wonderful to let other people see real kendo.

SENSEI: You know, Mr. Craig, one of my family years ago, Shusaku Chiba, you remember I told you one time he was credited for registering the Hokushin Itto Ryu style? Well, he was a promoter of exhibition matches before the common mass. These were exhibitions between the *naginata* and the sword.

CRAIG: Duels?

SENSEI: Yes.

CRAIG: Duels to the death, Sensei?

SENSEI: No. They used a mock *naginata* and a *shinai* similar to the ones we have today.

CRAIG: What's a *naginata*?

SENSEI: It is a pole weapon that has a long handle with a short or long blade on it. It was used by the samurai on the battlefield. Later, in Shusaku Chiba's time, because Japan had reached a peaceful state under the new emperor, the *naginata* became obsolete as a weapon of war. The *naginata* was turned over to the females of samurai clans and they used it in defense of their homes.

CRAIG: Did Shusaku Sensei charge money for these exhibitions?

SENSEI: Yes.

CRAIG: You know, Sensei, the more I learn about the Chiba family the more we seem to have in common.

SENSEI: What do you mean?

CRAIG: Well, your family put on shows or exhibitions for money, and my family, in the circus, did something very similar.

SENSEI: I never thought about it quite like that, but I guess you're correct.

CRAIG: Sensei, have you ever fought in a duel?

SENSEI: No one ever wins in a duel.

CRAIG: I know, but I was just wondering because of the large scar on your forehead.

SENSEI: That's a story of long ago.

CRAIG: Am I asking about something I shouldn't?

SENSEI: Don't you always?

CRAIG: I?

SENSEI: If you would like, I would be happy to help you with the kendo demonstration.

CRAIG: Thank you, Sensei.

1983

CRAIG: Sensei, some other kendo instructor told me this summer that in the All Japan Kendo Federation *kata* there is one Hokushin Itto Ryu *kata*. Is that true?

SENSEI: Well, number three, *sanbonme*, is very close, but I think everything has changed with time.

CRAIG: What do you mean?

SENSEI: Well, when the Japanese police were employing the top swordsmen around 1885 they decided to standardize *kendo kata* for police use. I believe my father told me that they did accept one of our *kata*.

CRAIG: Do you remember what it was called?

SENSEI: No, but I'll look it up for you in the dojo records when I go back to Japan.

CRAIG: I guess many famous swordsmen come from the Hokushin Itto Ryu?

SENSEI: Some, but a lot of old-style kendo schools had their share of famous swordsmen.

CRAIG: Can you recall any one samurai in particular?

SENSEI: Well, just before the turn of the century, about 1898 or '99, the Butokuden was formed in Kyoto.

CRAIG: What does "Butokuden" mean, Sensei?

SENSEI: Martial Hall or maybe Great Virtues Martial Hall. It is very hard to translate. Takaharu Naito Sensei, a student of Hokushin Itto Ryu, was known throughout Japan as a master swordsman and for his spirit in martial affairs. He was put in charge of the kendo section along with a student of Jigaro Kano, the founder of judo, by the name of Hijime Isogai Sensei.

CRAIG: Sensei, what did your father think of Jigaro Kano Sensei and his judo? Or as far as that goes, what do you think about it?

SENSEI: I don't know anything about either, but I can tell you this, *budo* is *budo*. Did you ever hear the story about one of Kano Sensei's students called Mifune? It is recorded in Japanese history that Mifune Sensei, a renowned world judo master, had reached such a degree of psychophysical unity with himself that one afternoon he put on a demonstration where, with nothing more than a silk handkerchief, he deflected a rifle bullet fired at him.

CRAIG: How can that be possible, Sensei?

SENSEI: One can accomplish anything if he has the correct training and proper discipline.

1984

CRAIG: Sensei, did you ever find out about the Hokushin Itto Ryu *kata* we talked about last year?

SENSEI: Yes. I brought a copy of the original ten *kata* of 1885.

1. Kyoshin Meichi Ryu: *kuraizume*
2. Asayama Ichiden Ryu: *aun*
3. Kurama Ryu: *henka*
4. Shindo Munen Ryu: *uchiotoshi*
5. Jikishinkage Ryu: *hasso*
6. Yagyu Shinkage Ryu: *hasetsu*
7. Richin Ryu: *makiotoshi*

8. Jigen Ryu: *ichini no tachi*
9. Hozan Ryu: *hachiten-giri*
10. Hokushin Itto Ryu: *kadan no tsuki*

The Hokushin Itto Ryu *kata* was for thrusting at the opponent's right eye. After the turn of the century it is my understanding that the *kata* were changed or modified to consist of twelve techniques, three with the *kodachi*, or short sword, and nine with the *odachi*, or long sword. From this *kata*'s beginning in the early 1900s to the present, it has been altered several times but basically continues in its modern form with seven *odachi* and three *kodachi* as the Zen Nihon Kendo Renmei [All Japan Kendo Federation] *kata*. These ten *kata* have been adopted by the International Kendo Federation as its standardization in its promotion for rank.

CRAIG: Do you think that testing for rank is important today?

SENSEI: I think testing is essential for the beginners so they can correct their basics. Testing also forces a person to test his technical, physical, and mental abilities.

CRAIG: What do you look for in testing a beginner?

SENSEI: Movement. Their movements should appear natural with proper *kamae* and *kime*.

CRAIG: *Kamae* and *kime*, Sensei, are the realization of the correct posture?

SENSEI: Yes. But always remember this important factor: too much of either is considered crude. My father always said it was like a fugu [puffer fish]. On the inside is only air but on the outside it's powerful looking and sharp. When you're a beginner, testing and achieving rank is most important. As you mature you find out that it only matters what you can do, not what others think you can do. Testing reveals a true image of ourselves to others. If you fail a test, you learn a great deal. If you pass, you learn a little. In life we find a continuous test of ourselves. If we have the discipline to correct our shortcomings, we can reach a state of contentment in our daily kendo practice.

CRAIG: What is the highest level of kendo in your way of thinking, Sensei?

SENSEI: One who walks hand in hand with his own God. God has given me the talent to do kendo. I have always felt that was his gift to me; therefore it is my responsibility to study hard so that, when I practice kendo, it transforms into a noble and elegant art, not a means of destruction. He is always watching, and I feel in my heart he expects me to do my best. If I accomplish this goal, he will appreciate my efforts and lend a helping hand.

CRAIG: Sensei, you make kendo sound almost like a religion.

SENSEI: No . . . kendo is not a religion, but it is interwoven with the Japanese religious beliefs. I feel the two are almost inseparable at times. This only means we can use kendo to discipline a pure heart and mind. If your intentions are good, you should have no trouble influencing others who might be interested in kendo as a way of life.

CRAIG: When you talk of God, Sensei—and I do not wish to get into a religious discussion—

SENSEI: That's good.

CRAIG: —but isn't Zen a religion for martial arts or adopted by the samurai for their warring ways?

SENSEI: Yes. Zen had a profound influence on the samurai's role and their *bushido,* or moral code of conduct, especially as it pertained to religious and spiritual development. Their martial arts training was more often spent in physical development than in spiritual meditation, whereas the training of a Zen priest would be just the opposite. The samurai was known to spend a great deal of time in Zen temples meditating. This enabled him to expel all fear of death through the elimination of his ego. Without his ego, he found little if any suffering or fear of the unknown, such as death. Through meditation, his mind and body were eventually prepared to meet death under any circumstances with a peaceful spirit. According to the Zen beliefs, when the body dies the ego also dies. This enabled the samurai to look at death without experiencing the actual physical death of a person. Do you understand anything I have said?

CRAIG: You got me, Sensei.

SENSEI: Got me? What's that mean?

CRAIG: It means I don't have the slightest idea of what you're talking about.

SENSEI: Good! I'm still holding the candle. Remember, it's your job to find the footholds. I have patience and will have lunch while you're pondering.

1985

CRAIG: Sensei, I just thought of something.

SENSEI: All by yourself?

CRAIG: Well, I think so.

SENSEI: That's good. What's your question?

CRAIG: How did you know it was going to be a question?

SENSEI: Just a guess, I suppose.

CRAIG: OK. My question is this: If you're a descendent of the Chiba family after thirty-seven generations of more than seven hundred and fifty years (and I am in no way questioning that, believe me), does that mean there has always been a male to carry on the blood line, generation after generation?

SENSEI: That is correct.

CRAIG: Well, that's just remarkable.

SENSEI: There is no limit to what a man can do with discipline, hard work, and perseverance.

CRAIG: Sensei, have you ever thought about why you accepted me as your student?

SENSEI: Now, that is a good question . . . Just kidding, Mr. Craig. I accepted your mind, at first, not your body.

CRAIG: I don't understand.

SENSEI: Well, a person's mind contains impressions of all the bad and all the good actions in that person's present and past lives. Only a select few individuals have the ability to recall these impressions. The actions one takes in his present life reflect the conditions of one's future lives. The mind influences every action of the body. No action of the body can be made without the consent of either the conscious or subconscious. When we first met, I felt nothing but good impressions from your subconscious, no guilt or remorse. With this in mind, I accepted you as my student. I must add that there are times when you need a sharp slap on the back with a thin stick to wake up your subconscious. Nothing we all don't need from time to time.

CRAIG: Thank you, Sensei.

SENSEI: Of course, you must keep in mind also that I didn't know you were so inquisitive in your past lives.

CRAIG: Is there anything else you look for when accepting a new student?

SENSEI: A student of kendo should come to the dojo as a sheet of paper comes to a Japanese calligrapher, perfectly clean and blank, waiting for the master's brush, receiving each stroke of the brush and absorbing all the ink it takes to make the perfect line. Even to a master Zen calligrapher the numeral "one" is the hardest to make. And in life we all start with the numeral one, master and student alike. I think, too, a student, old or new, should never make excuses when being corrected. We all make mistakes. It is the *sensei's* duty to see when the student is unable to find the next foothold and hold the light a little closer. It is important to know just how close to hold the light. If you hold it too close, you will burn the student and he will let go and fall. If you bring the light each time he cries out for help, he will never learn to do for himself. I guess you could sum it up by saying, to be and remain a good student you should follow without question. Listen very carefully to everything the teacher has to say whether you understand it now or not.

CRAIG: Sensei?

SENSEI: What?

CRAIG: That was great!

SENSEI: I know. But I'm not being very humble. Sometimes, Mr. Craig, you bring out the worst in me.

CRAIG: I'm sorry, Sensei. I don't mean to.

SENSEI: Sometimes I think you ask enough questions to fill a book.

CRAIG: I'm trying, Sensei.

SENSEI: God help the reader. I hope we're both just kidding.

CRAIG: Well, Sensei, I might someday.

SENSEI: Might what?

CRAIG: Write a book.

SENSEI: *No!!!*

CRAIG: Would you mind?

SENSEI: Mind what?

CRAIG: If I wrote a book.

SENSEI: About what?

CRAIG: What we talk about and the way you give instruction.

SENSEI: Will I get a signed copy?

CRAIG: Of course, if you'll sign one for me.

SENSEI: What for? You are the one doing all the writing.

CRAIG: Yes, Sensei, but you are the tree. I am nothing more than the wind forcing you to let go of a few leaves.

SENSEI: Say, that sounds like me.

CRAIG: Really?

SENSEI: How long have we known each other now?

CRAIG: About six or seven years.

SENSEI: Maybe you're learning a little too fast. It's not good to overteach.

CRAIG: What do you mean?

SENSEI: Nothing. Just a thought that seemed to escape through my lips.

CRAIG: Sensei?

SENSEI: [no answer]

CRAIG: Sensei, what do you think is the number one problem with kendo today?

SENSEI: Probably that students try to learn too fast. The sword must make a perfect circle around the body without exception. This should take about ten years. Nowadays I feel a lot of teachers put more emphasis on winning—not that there is anything wrong in winning, but everything must be kept in its correct perspective. If you practice kendo each day for the final duel tomorrow and each evening you put all your affairs in order, and if with the light of the new day you go out to meet your opponent but he never appears, then you are doing proper kendo. There is an old samurai saying: "Sharpen your sword every day and wash your neck before you go to bed, pray to God each night that there will be no war tomorrow."

CRAIG: Do you think that kendo changes us, Sensei?

SENSEI: No. Kendo cannot change you. Only you can change yourself.

1986

CRAIG: Sensei, when I was at the *hombu* dojo last year one of the students was telling me that the Hokushin Itto Ryu had a dojo song. Is that true?

SENSEI: Yes.

CRAIG: Can you tell me how it came about?

SENSEI: The story as told to me goes something like this. In about 1850 or so a young man came for instruction to Naito Takaharu Sensei, who was a master teacher of the Hokushin Itto Ryu style. He became a member of the Chiba clan. Unfortunately, he also became *yakuza*, so after several years, he left the dojo.

CRAIG: Sensei, what's *yakuza*?

SENSEI: Well, *yakuza* are like gangsters, but in the old days a lot of them were like what you would call Robin Hood.

CRAIG: Robin Hood? You mean they stole from the rich and gave to the poor?

SENSEI: Well maybe one or two did. Most of them stole from everybody and gave to themselves. Once he left the Chiba dojo and became *yakuza*, no matter how much good he might have done, he could never return to the dojo's way. In his maturing years he felt so much remorse over his youthful decision to leave the Chiba way that he wrote a song that became very popular among the *yakuza* clans. I guess you could call what he wrote a folk song similar to your Western music—full of tears and sorrows.

CRAIG: Sensei, do you know the song?

SENSEI: Of course. I think everyone in the dojo is familiar with it.

CRAIG: I'm not.

SENSEI: Well, I'll try and remember to bring a copy next time.

CRAIG: Thank you. Will it be in Japanese?

SENSEI: Of course. It's a Japanese song. If you tried to translate it I think you would lose much of the true meaning.

CRAIG: OK. I'll learn it in Japanese, but you'll have to explain it to me for my son.

SENSEI: That's good.

CRAIG: Sensei, during the Edo period did the Chiba dojo have a prominent member?

SENSEI: Well, quite a few, but the one I'll tell you about is Eijiro Chiba (1832–62). He became famous throughout Japan for his *katate jodan no kamae* (one-handed over-the-head posture). He had an uncanny way of locating an opening in his opponent's defense and striking furiously with a whiplike motion. I don't believe he was ever beaten in a match. Though he used a *shinai*, his cutting action was always *ippatsu*.

CRAIG: What does that mean, Sensei?

SENSEI: It's hard to explain, but in English the best explanation would be to cut the opponent as with a real sword, not simply touching him. This was referred to back then as the positive style of fencing.

CRAIG: Sensei, Eijiro Chiba was a relatively young man—if your figures are correct, about thirty years old. Isn't that kind of unusual to die so young even back then? Was he killed in a duel?

SENSEI: I don't know. I'll have to look it up.

1987

CRAIG: Sensei, looking at my notes from our conversation last year, I was wondering if you brought a copy of the Chiba song?

SENSEI: Well, Sensei, I—

CRAIG: Who are you talking to?

SENSEI: You. Why?

CRAIG: You never called me *sensei* before.

SENSEI: Does that surprise you?

CRAIG: Well, I don't know quite what to say.

SENSEI: That proves it.

CRAIG: Proves what, Sensei?

SENSEI: That it's time to call you Sensei.

CRAIG: I guess. I never thought of myself as a *sensei* like you . .

SENSEI: You're not like me, and I don't want you to be. Do you know what *sensei* means?

CRAIG: Well, I always thought it meant "teacher."

SENSEI: In Japan it has come to mean that. But the word *sensei* is made from two ideograms that may be translated as "one who is born before."

CRAIG: Before what, Sensei?

SENSEI: Before his students. Don't you have students?

CRAIG: Yes.

SENSEI: Well, are any of them older than you?

CRAIG: No, I don't think so.

SENSEI: Then you are their *sensei*. In the Hokushin Itto Ryu, I am what the Japanese call *sei*—and before you ask, it means one who is a lineal descendant of head masters from a *ryu* or martial arts line. Just as my father was, my sons are, and their sons are, you have been and are now my *monjin* [disciple]. But in my mind, even though you are my *monjin*, you are also a *sensei*. When you were practicing in my dojo the last time, I placed your name and your son's name in the *ryu's* book as *hatamoto* [banner men].

CRAIG: You have bestowed a great honor on my family, Sensei. Thank you.

SENSEI: It is a moral responsibility I place on you, Craig Sensei. You now have to hold up my teachings in an undistorted fashion. Always remember: when you wear the mark, you carry the burden. But in the past years I have come to know you to be of rigid discipline and dedicated to the cultivation of *budo*. You and I will travel far in our quest.

CRAIG: I hope so, Sensei.

SENSEI: Craig Sensei, I brought you some information about the Chiba family. Shusaku Chiba of the Edo era was a master swordsman. He was extremely powerful and a rather large man by Japanese standards. It is written in the family hand scrolls.

CRAIG: Sensei, are they the ones you showed me one time upstairs over the dojo?

SENSEI: Yes. Anyway, he wrote that the soul of swordsmanship lies in the excellence of technique and not in the physical force of a man. He had four main points to his teaching.

CRAIG: And they were, Sensei?

SENSEI: I'm getting to that, if you'd just have a little patience.

1. Always use a straight *bokuto*. Use nothing with knots or curvature.
2. When confronting the enemy, always walk in a natural manner. Take whatever number of steps the *maai* [distance between opponents] requires.
3. Never make any noise when moving, but move freely anytime, anyplace in an efficient manner.
4. Always use the *onikote*.

CRAIG: What kind of *kote* were those, Sensei?

SENSEI: They were extremely large. They protected your complete forearm and hand, which allowed you to practice full cutting action.

CRAIG: Sensei, how far back do those hand scrolls go?

SENSEI: They have been in the Chiba family for several centuries. Some are so old they have become brittle and faded, making them difficult if not impossible to read.

CRAIG: Do you know any other writings from the scrolls by heart, Sensei?

SENSEI: Well let's see . . . no, not that I can think of now.

CRAIG: What is the difference in your mind, Sensei, between kendo and *kenjitsu*?

SENSEI: The difference between the two arts sits before you. There is a great difference between *bujutsu* and *budo*. *Bujutsu* means martial arts, while *budo* means martial way. *Bujutsu* was a system designed by samurai such as the Hokushin Itto Ryu family for the protection of family solidarity. While *budo*, like kendo, is a spiritual system, *budo* was not necessarily designed by samurai or for warriors. At one time in Japan's martial arts, they were taught for self-protection, but in Japan today *budo* is taught for self-perfection. Basically, *kenjitsu* was developed during Japan's martial activity period, while *budo* came much, much later. But always remember: when building something new, you must learn from the past.

CRAIG: Then what I learn in kendo is not a fighting art?

SENSEI: No. I didn't say that exactly. If you wish to use kendo as a fighting art you can, but it is not *kenjitsu*. When you practice *kata*, then you are practicing *kenjitsu*. It is designed from *bujutsu* to be used by *budo* people practicing kendo. Understand?

CRAIG: Yes. Through *kata* we have a window to the past.

SENSEI: Exactly. The Chiba family's *kata* are *kenjitsu*, centuries old, yet we still practice them with the new *budo* of kendo.

CRAIG: That's pretty neat, Sensei.

SENSEI: I'm glad you like it.

CRAIG: Sensei, when does a teacher become a master of kendo?

SENSEI: Well, that is a very good question. The Japanese answer would be simple.

CRAIG: That's OK. I'm a simple student.

SENSEI: In Japan, if a teacher called himself a master, then he is considered so usually in title only. My father always said, "My master is dead, and when I die, I'll be your master. For now I'm just your father and will instruct you in the correct way." In my way of thinking, a master in *budo* should be able to keep his student on the uphill climb yet allow him to rest—not changing his good side, but guiding the bad side to safety.

CRAIG: Sensei, what does *shihan* mean?

SENSEI: "Master teacher" is its accepted meaning in Japan. But personally I feel it is the most misunderstood and overused word in the Japanese language, especially in foreign countries.

CRAIG: Why is that, Sensei?

SENSEI: *Shihan* is a term used in old dojos to show respect to students who support the dojo and help point the correct way. It does not always mean that the person is a master of martial arts. The word itself comes from ancient China. Chinese legend tells of a type of compass called a *shinansha*. The *shinansha* compass points faithfully in the direction a traveler should follow. The *shinansha* was a statue mounted on a wagon with its arm upraised and pointed in a southward direction. The Chinese used it to guide them in the right direction. In Japan hundreds of years ago, when the martial arts were in their infancy, the Japanese took the word *shinansha* and changed the kanji to read *shihan*, which literally translates "to finger south." It is used to identify the instructor or person who, like the Chinese compass, always pointed toward the right direction.

1988

SENSEI: Craig Sensei, is there something bothering you?

CRAIG: No. Why?

SENSEI: Well, I've been here for two days and this is the first time you've brought out your recorder.

CRAIG: It's just that I've been so busy with the government, teaching, and everything, I haven't had time to put down the questions as usual.

SENSEI: Maybe you're running out of questions, or you're getting older, like me, and questions are not as important as they used to be.

CRAIG: We are getting older, Sensei, there isn't any doubt about that. But there are a couple of questions that I'd like to ask. They're on more of a personal level, though.

SENSEI: You can always ask. That doesn't necessarily mean you'll get the answer you are looking for.

CRAIG: Well, Sensei, I have always wondered about the large knot on your right wrist. How did you come by it?

SENSEI: Practicing kendo.

CRAIG: Did you get your wrist broken?

SENSEI: No, nothing so easy as that. It's from being hit on the *kote* too often. In my father's day it was common to see a kendo instructor with such a . . . what did you call it, a knot?

CRAIG: Yes.

SENSEI: The old *sensei* of kendo used to have their kimonos made so the sleeves would go down to the middle of their hands. That way, it wouldn't show when they were out in public.

CRAIG: Why was that, Sensei?

SENSEI: To keep the common people from knowing they were kendo teachers and maybe starting some kind of trouble. Anyway, that's what my father said. My father's knot was almost even with the top of the thumb when his fist was closed.

CRAIG: Sensei, that's a lot of hits on the *kote*.

SENSEI: Yes, but what better way to learn a *waza* than to feel the incorrect way first? The way one used to train in *bujutsu* is quite different from the way we train now.

1989

CRAIG: Sensei, what should I think about when practicing kendo?

SENSEI: Nothing.

CRAIG: Nothing?

SENSEI: Yes, nothing. You cannot express the feelings of sorrow and joy at the same time. Neither can you think and practice kendo. If you do, you are still on the lowest level of the mountain path. Like when you teach, you cannot express the feelings of sorrow and joy to another person. They are merely words. One must experience them to understand their true meaning. Oh, sometimes words can help you up the path and guide you for a short distance in the right direction, but the ultimate test is the person himself. The correct decision on what to do at the correct time while practicing is within you and nowhere else. This is where your discipline with basics appears. Only you hold the key to your mind.

CRAIG: Sensei, can you tell me what a master of kendo like yourself sees in another master kendoist?

SENSEI: I'm not a master.

CRAIG: Sorry, Sensei. I—

SENSEI: That's all right. One teacher looks to see if the other teacher is ahead of him or behind him on the mountain. If he is ahead, he looks for hand- and footholds he has left.

CRAIG: And if he is behind, Sensei?

SENSEI: He does nothing.

CRAIG: Sensei, do you think there are any secrets in kendo?

SENSEI: No. The only secrets in kendo—or as far as that goes, in anything—is hard work. Secrets are for fools. Kendo is made up of two things, discipline and practice. One is no good without the other. What good is it to show you a new *waza* if you haven't practiced the last one? I cannot teach you anything, I can only show you. You must teach yourself. If I show you some kind of trick in kendo, it is only good for one or two times or until someone else sees it. Then he can practice a defense against it. You will gain false confidence from it and lose your footing and start sliding down the path. If I were to tell you everything that I know and have learned in my life about *budo* or kendo, what good would it be to you? It becomes worth something only when you discover it for yourself. Take a small child, if you tell him not to touch the boiling pot or he will burn himself, the only thing he hears is *do not*. So naturally sooner or later he will have to find out for himself. When you master a particular *waza* in kendo your opponent will appear at the end of your sword so close you will not have to cut him. He will cut himself. This is where the proper *kiai* comes in.

CRAIG: I don't understand, Sensei.

SENSEI: When the opponent is this close your *kiai* will force him to react improperly and he will be cut.

CRAIG: Sensei, I find it hard to make a student understand the *kiai's* importance.

SENSEI: That's only natural. Most people think it comes from the brain, but in truth, if it is properly executed, it comes from the inner strength of the stomach just below the navel. This is called *tanden* in Japanese. The proper *kiai* can appear only if the mind is not activated to make improper movements of the body. The mind must be in a complete state of *muga*.

CRAIG: What is *muga*?

SENSEI: Here again is one of those Japanese words that has many definitions and is extremely hard to translate. I feel it is best explained by saying the mind is in a state of complete void or emptiness, a state of no ego . . . Are you following me, Craig Sensei?

CRAIG: Yes, I think so. You're saying when your practice becomes subconscious instead of conscious?

SENSEI: You are on the correct path. This *muga* is the state of mind all kendoists hope to obtain eventually but seldom do. When a student reaches this level in his practice he has no thought of defeat or victory. He is not afraid of death and there is no anger in his heart, only peace.

CRAIG: Well, I know one thing for sure, Sensei. I'm scared as hell when I practice *ippon shobu* with you.

SENSEI: Yes, I know, Craig Sensei, but your mind is not *muga*. You still wish your mind to protect your body in the face of danger. It is only natural for you to still have a partial ego to command your body to react. This is called *munen-muso*, a mind where there is no contention or malice, just a desire to protect the body.

CRAIG: I don't know, Sensei. Sometimes when we are practicing, I feel like wetting my pants.

SENSEI: I would say then you are overreacting. But getting back to *kiai*, I have heard my father talk about samurai who developed such a strong *kiai* from the lower abdomen it would off-balance their opponent in combat. A samurai of this stature could split a stalk of rice with a single stroke of his sword or cut down flies in midflight.

1990

CRAIG: Sensei, I know some students of kendo who can hit their target's *kote*, *men*, or *do* consistently, but they have poor form and bend at the waist.

SENSEI: What is your question, Craig Sensei?

CRAIG: Well, how can they have such poor form and still have such accuracy to hit their mark?

SENSEI: They hardly ever change and, in my way of thinking, they're at the part of the path that says "Start" and is the lowest form of kendo. Don't you think it's better to concentrate on timing, balance, posture, and correct technique than just being able to hit a target with the speed you de-

3
THE REI

THE first thing a new student is shown in a traditional Japanese dojo is to bow, or *rei*. He discovers himself bowing to this and bowing to that, bowing to enter, bowing to leave. In fact, the new student usually starts bowing to everything. Why is it required in traditional Japanese martial arts to *rei* to a wall, to a picture, to the *kamiza* (shrine), to the *sensei*, to our partner, upon entering and leaving the dojo, when sitting or standing? I'll try to explain.

First of all, to *rei* properly is an art in itself, requiring time and training. Few Westerners bow correctly. Perhaps they feel it is undemocratic, or a religious gesture, or an indication of obsequious submission. It is not. It is merely a demonstration of respect. Most people study martial arts to learn discipline and to try to lose their ego. A student who cannot *rei* without these negative feelings hasn't a chance of obtaining what martial arts has to offer.

Before addressing the bow itself, however, let's address two fundamental items: how to sit in the dojo and how to breathe properly.

SEIZA

Seiza is a way of sitting on the knees that is used extensively in *budo*, in some dojos to reinforce discipline. We sit in *seiza* at the beginning and end of each traditional Japanese martial art class. To sit in *seiza*, bend your legs and place your left knee on the floor while keeping the ball and the toes of your left foot on the floor. Your left knee should be in line with your right foot. Now slide your right foot to the rear, toes on the floor, until your right knee is on the floor. Your knees will be in line with each other: approximately two fists apart for men, and as close together as possible for women. Your toes can now slide back so that your insteps are on the floor. At this point cross your right big toe over your left big toe. Lower your hips and buttocks so that they rest slightly on top of and between your heels. Many old *sensei* don't cross their toes but rather place the instep of the right foot on the sole of the left foot. As the years have gone by, I have learned why: the calluses on the top of the feet grow large, and when they break open or peel off, you automatically place one foot on top of the other to ease the pain.

It is important to stay as relaxed as possible in *seiza*. Try to relax the shoulders and the buttocks, and keep the spine slightly relaxed with a small S-shaped curve. Your head should be tilted slightly forward, your ears in line with your shoulders, and your nose in line with the center of your stomach. Your body weight should be centered somewhere between the soles of your feet and your knees. Finding this center point will help to prevent cramping. O Sensei said, "When I was a child, my father used to take the topknot on my head and pull straight upward and tell me as he released the pressure to allow my body to flow downward and settle naturally between my feet and knees." Your eyes should be half-closed and focused on a spot about three feet in front of you. Hold the teeth slightly together while placing the tongue on the roof of your mouth to help cut down the need to swallow.

Until about 1955 the only way to sit in a dojo was in *seiza*. As the years passed, sitting in *anza* became acceptable; that is, cross-legged American Indian style. It is important to note that *anza* is acceptable in the dojo only when the instructor allows it. Whether you're in *seiza* or in *anza* it is important to keep the legs folded close to your body.

Sitting in *seiza* probably arose from the tradition of never looking down on the *sensei*. In the old dojos the *sensei* would sit on a small platform near the Shinto shrine. This place of honor allowed the *sensei* to be a little above the students during the *rei*. It also allowed him to keep a close eye on everyone. If you were to approach the *sensei* after practice, for example, to ask a question, he again would be just a little higher than the student. This made him invulnerable to a surprise attack, as he would be if he were at eye level with the student.

Sitting in *seiza* or *anza* also provides more space in the dojo. Because space has long been at a premium in Japan, it is considered rude to occupy more of it than needed. Also to be considered is the safety element; a student whose arms and legs are sprawled out all over the place risks injuring not only himself but also another student.

BREATHING

Breathing properly can be broken down into three phases: inhaling, retaining, and exhaling. Inhaling, or taking air into the lungs, should always be natural and never forced or hurried. Never gulp. The amount of air you take in should always be according to the needs of the body at that particular moment. Retaining is probably the least thought of but most important element of breathing. During the retention phase the energies are built up for their release in the exhalation phase. In martial arts the exhalation should be tied into the *kiai* or with the cut of the sword, *kote*, or other weapon. With the exhalation your internal energy is released. Not all the air should be released from the lungs. This leaves you breath for the *zanshin*, or alertness after an attack, so important in martial arts.

While breathing should be natural, it is also done in a specific manner. Inhale through the nose and exhale through the slightly parted lips, using the diaphragm. Only the abdomen should move while breathing. Inhale quietly, not allowing the shoulders to rise and fall with each breath. Breathe softly and allow the abdomen to move naturally with each inhalation and exhalation. If you watch a baby lying on its back in a crib, you will notice that only the abdomen extends and contracts with each breath. This is a natural way to breathe.

The ancient Chinese believed that each soul was allotted only so many breaths. To waste a breath was a sin and shortened one's life; conversely, to breathe slowly and naturally prolonged life. The average person inhales and exhales about fifteen or sixteen times every minute, thus inhaling and exhaling once every three to four seconds, or approximately twenty-three thousand breaths in a twenty-four-hour period. Interestingly, animals that breathe very slowly, such as the tortoise, tend to live very long lives.

Most people breathe incorrectly and are unaware of it. On the other hand, if you are a jogger or a runner you probably breath correctly but may be unaware of the reason. The easiest way to check yourself for proper breathing is to place your right hand lightly on the center of your abdomen just below the solar plexus. Without changing your normal breathing pattern, see if the stomach noticeably extends on the inhale and contracts on the exhale. If you're breathing with your chest and not the diaphragm, the opposite will occur. One great exercise that opera singers of the Italian bel canto tradition use to regulate their breathing involves lying flat on your back on the floor and relaxing. Take a large book and place it on your stomach someplace comfortable between your chest and pelvis. Now place a glass of water (not too full) on top of the book. As the diaphragm begins to work, the book will rise and fall with each breath. When you are lying on the floor this way, your spine is straight, encouraging you to breathe with the diaphragm instead of the chest. By keeping the spine straight when practicing kendo, you will not only be able to breathe properly but also have much more endurance. I think this is why O Sensei always wanted me to squeeze my buttocks together when practicing: it helped keep my spine straight. Even then, he reminded me of the importance of keeping the rest of the body completely relaxed.

THE SITTING REI

The *rei* should be performed no less politely whether you're sitting or standing. When sitting, *rei* only from the *seiza* position; it is considered impolite to *rei* from the *anza*. When bowing from the sitting position, the left hand should leave your side first, followed immediately by the right. The hands should make a triangle in front of your body. The hands should be far enough in front of you so that you can place your nose in the center of the triangle. This should be accomplished without your buttocks leaving your heels and without exposing the back of your neck to the person to whom you are bowing.

Both the sitting and the standing *rei* are described in greater detail in chapter 8.

THE STANDING REI

One of the most imitated and the least understood of all martial art rituals, especially in the West, is the standing *rei*. It is important to keep in mind that shaking hands or touching each other in any form, from slapping someone on the back to seizing his elbow, is a Western custom considered impolite among the Japanese. While the Japanese may have accepted these Western gestures for business reasons, they have not in *budo*. There it is still considered rude, with predictable consequences.

The standing *rei* is done by bending from the waist, heels together, feet angled at an approximate forty-five-degree angle, your head tilted slightly upward so as not to lose eye contact with whomever or whatever you're bowing to. Allow your hands to slide forward in front of your legs, fingers pointing down while the hands slide down your thighs toward your knees. The lower the bow, the more the respect; however, you should never allow your fingers to go below the tops of your knees. Keep your back straight and do not hold the *rei* too long; usually a slow count of three is sufficient. Do not bob your head up and down.

It appalls me to see someone slapping his sides when performing a standing *rei*, an outlandish behavior we can credit to the moviemakers. It is incorrect and, in my way of thinking, shows disrespect to the arts. Also, once you have stepped on the dojo floor it is important that your posture show attention and respect. Thus it is impolite to do such things as put your hands in your *obi* (sash), slouch against a wall, or stand with your legs crossed.

THE REI WHEN ENTERING OR LEAVING

In traditional Japanese dojos it is customary to bow when entering or leaving the dojo. This is done with a standing bow, to show respect to the *sensei* and to all those who have gone before you on the quest for perfection. Chiba Sensei told me that the *rei* when entering the dojo was to remind the student that he was entering the *sensei's* world and to leave the outside world outside. This is the first step up the endless mountain path of knowledge. How can a student unwilling to show respect to the guide expect to be shepherded on his journey? To bow when leaving the dojo thanks the *sensei* for his guidance and returns the student to the confused world outside the *sensei*'s walls. The *rei* when entering and leaving the dojo is similar to knocking on someone's door. The person comes to the door and asks what you want. You reply, "Instruction," and are allowed to enter. Afterward you thank the person, shake hands, and leave. All this is done in the *sensei*'s house with the simple *rei*.

THE SHINZEN REI

At the beginning of each session the class is required to bow generally two or three times. In most dojos the first *rei* is performed toward the high point in the dojo, where a photograph of the founder of the art or the particular dojo's style is hanging. This *shinzen rei* shows respect to the founder and says that, as students of his style or *ryu*, we are going to practice hard and try to follow his principles.

Some dojos hang not a photograph but a scroll, which may be changed with the seasons. The scroll represents the heart of the dojo and gives the student a sense of connection with the past, especially if the scroll is in the founder's own hand. The scroll usually has a martial art saying on it, such as "Wind, forest, fire, mountain," which signifies an old samurai saying: "We come like the wind, we are as quiet as the forest, we are as thorough as fire, and once we conquer we are as immovable as a mountain." Chiba Sensei once gave me such a scroll. It reads:

Kiri mosubu-tachi-no-soita koso
Gigoku-nare
Mio sutete koso ukabu se mo-are

This is an old Miyamoto Musashi saying: "Under the Issoku Itto, distance is dangerous. You have to step forward, as it is safer."

The *rei* to the photograph or scroll is done in the *seiza* position most of the time. I have been to some dojos, not in Japan, where the students stand and *rei*. Keep in mind that each instructor will have his or her own way of starting and ending a class, and some Western instructors have established a distinct code of behavior when doing so.

The second *rei* is to the present *sensei*. It shows that we respect him and trust him to teach us what he has learned.

In some old *ryu* such as the Hokushin Chiba Itto Ryu there are three *rei*: two as I have already explained, and a third from the *sensei* to the student. Master Chiba always said, "Three is a good way. I bow to my father, who was my teacher. You bow to me because I am your teacher, and I must bow once to you as my student. After I am gone you must carry on all that I have taught you. For this I must show you respect. It always takes three to keep the *ryu* alive. Someday you will bow to me when I am no longer in this body as your teacher. Your students and son will bow to you as their teacher. You must always bow to your son and students with the greatest respect, for someday your son will take your place and the whole process will start over again. We as martial artists are very lucky to have sons to carry on the work we have started. Some people do not, so they must search for one person whom they can trust to carry on their teachings."

THE REI TO THE SHINTO SHRINE

Shinto, the indigenous religion of Japan, goes back at least two thousand years. Its written literature, however, dates back only to the *Nihongi* (Chronicles of Japan) and *Kojiki* (Records of Ancient Matters), written in 712 and 720 CE, respectively, and traditionally attributed to the Emperor Temmu. These two books, the closest thing Shinto has to official scripture, combine the history of Japan with ancient mythology handed down orally. Together they establish the ancestral and nature worship that constitutes Shinto, the "Way of the *Kami*." According to Shinto, everything on Earth—a mountain, an animal or a tree—has *kami*, which is usually translated as spirit or life force and may be personified as a deity. A mountain, such as Mount Fuji, is inhabited by a *kami*, which can also act as a protector for those who live near or on it.

Buddhism, since its introduction into Japan in the sixth century CE, has influenced Shinto beliefs, although Shinto remains a distinct religion. Ryobu (Dual Aspect) Shinto, which arose during the Kamakura period (1185–1392) and incorporates concepts from Shingon (True Word) Buddhism, has, along with Zen, shaped the tenets of *bushido*, or the way of the warrior. Ryobu Shinto beliefs are simple: the present moment is the only reality. There is no concept of punishment or reward after death. The Kamakura shoguns, who stressed the importance of mental and bodily disciplines, found in Ryobu Shinto the perfect belief system for a samurai: respect for ancestors and teachers, along with the lesson that you must practice for now, and as hard as you can, because tomorrow or even the next minute does not exist.

The Shinto shrine in the dojo represents these beliefs and deserves the respect of all martial artists, whether or not they consider themselves followers of Shinto. I always envision the *rei* to the shrine as another transitional step from the outside world to the world of my *sensei's* traditions. Bowing to the shrine allows me to reflect on the history of his art and express my gratitude to its founder and previous instructors, who are so interwoven with my life.

THE REI TO THE SENSEI

The *rei* to the *sensei* should be done at the beginning and end of each class. It shows a willingness to learn, a request to be instructed, and your gratitude for his patience in instructing you.

If the *sensei* instructs you personally during a class, you should give a small but polite *rei*. This shows him that you are paying attention to his instruction. When he is finished you should *rei* again. This indicates that you understand his instruction and will try to do better.

THE REI TO YOUR PARTNER

A *rei* to your partner at the beginning and end of your work together shows respect to the person who is willing to practice with you. As with all the other types of *rei* discussed in this chapter, it is a part of good etiquette in the dojo, not a form of submission. Manners are not an add-on; they are part of the art.

4

KENDO EQUIPMENT

THIS chapter addresses the equipment used in kendo: what it is, how to put it on and take it off correctly, and how to care for it. The armor used in kendo, called the *bogu*, is based on the traditional *yoroi* of the samurai, as can be seen in the photographs on this page and the next.

The *yoroi* comprises eight basic pieces of equipment. The *kabuto-etchu-zunari-bachi* (1), or helmet bowl, is of simple construction, with a longitudinal top plate overlapping the brow plate. The *hoate*, or *mengu* (2), sometimes called the face armor, consists of a mask that covers the chin and the cheeks. It is at times worn with the *nodawa*, an additional piece of armor that protects the throat and upper chest. The *sode* (3) are the shoulder guards. The *shintogote* (4) are sleeve and hand protectors worn under the *sode*. The *yukinoshitado* (5) is a body protector that covers the front and back; it is externally hinged, usually on the left side, and tied on the right, although in rare cases it is hinged in the front and tied in the back. The *hodohaidate* (6) are thigh protectors, attached to the

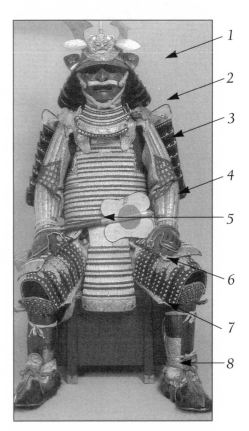

The yoroi, or old-style samurai armor.

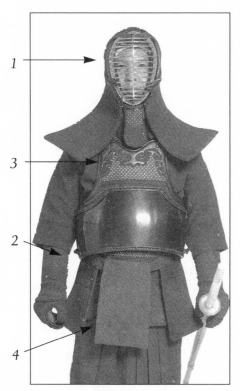

The bogu, or armor used in present-day kendo

lower part of the *yukinoshitado* and divided into pendant sections. The *ikadahaidate* (7), worn under the *hodohaidate*, afford an apronlike defense for the thighs. Lastly, the *shinosuneate* (8), or shin guards, are splints connected by mail; some are hinged in the center to avoid rubbing the instep. (In *naginatado*, practice using a pole weapon with a long blade, the *shinosuneate* are simply called *suneate*, and both sides of the legs are targets, along with the *men, do, kote,* and *tsuki.*) An additional piece of protection, which is considered an accessory and is not pictured here, is the *wakibiki*, a guard for the armpits that can be worn with or without armor.

The armor used in kendo today bears certain similarities with the *yoroi*. The *men* (1), which protects the head, throat, face, and shoulder, replaces the *kabuto, hoate, nodawa,* and *sode* found in the older armor. The *kote* (2) is the hand and wrist protector. When *kenjitsu* changed to kendo and the search for spiritual perfection replaced the perfection of battlefield skills, the arms were no longer a target, only the wrists; accordingly, the *kote* replaced the *shinogote*. The *do* (3) is a body protector with an open back. As with the *kote*, the back is no longer a target; it is considered bad manners to strike from behind. Thus the *do* replaces the *yukinoshitado,* and the targets are limited to right and left side cuts and to the solar plexus or chest for *tsuki*. Lastly, the *tare* (4) is a thigh, hip, and groin protector that replaces the *hodohaidate* and the *ikadahaidate*. Although the groin is not a legitimate target in kendo, it must be protected in case of an accident, such as with the thrusting motions of *tsuki*. The *tare* provides this protection, as well as additional padding for the *do* when doing *taiatari*. Because leg cuts are not permitted in kendo, the *shinosuneate*, or shin guards, are no longer used. A student who desires to practice with shin guards, however, can always purchase a pair of *naginata suneate*. I might add that participating with a good naginataist, as I once did, is a humbling experience.

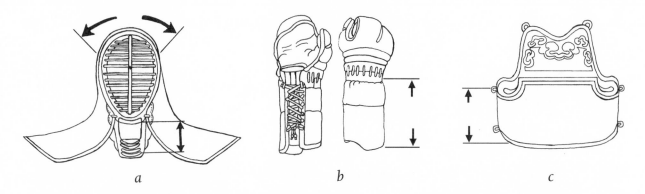

Figure 4.1 illustrates the locations of the legitimate cuts in kendo. The drawing of the *men* (fig. 4.1*a*) shows two areas. The upper arrow indicates the area of the three proper cuts to the head: *shomen-uchi,* to the center of the head; *migi-men-uchi,* right side of the head; and *hidari-men-uchi,* to the left side of the head. The lower arrow shows the area of proper thrusts against the throat, which can be performed *tsuki,* which is a two-handed thrust, or *katate-tsuki,* a one-handed thrust. The drawing of the *kote* (fig. 4.1*b*) indicates where a proper *kote-uchi* can be delivered—to the top of the right wrist of an opponent in *chudan-no-kamae* position, and to the bottom of the left wrist of an opponent in *jodan-no-kamae.* The drawing of the *do* (fig. 4.1*c*) shows the location of proper body cuts: the *migi-do-uchi,* or cut to the right side, and *hidari-do-uchi,* or cut to the left side. Although the left *do* is a target, it is seldom scored in a tournament, because to cut the *do* properly is extremely difficult and leaves your *men* and *kote* open for attack. Right *do* is attempted more often but is still difficult to score. Traditionally, the left side was not struck as often because the samurai wore his swords on that side. As already explained, there are no legitimate cuts to the *tare* (fig. 4.1*d*). All of the cutting is done with the first five or six inches of the *shinai* (fig. 4.1*e*).

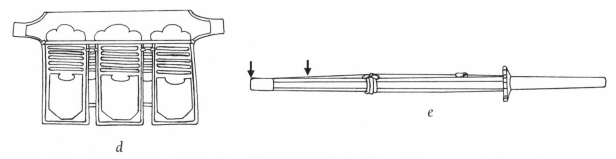

FIGURE 4.1. *The locations of the legitimate cuts.*

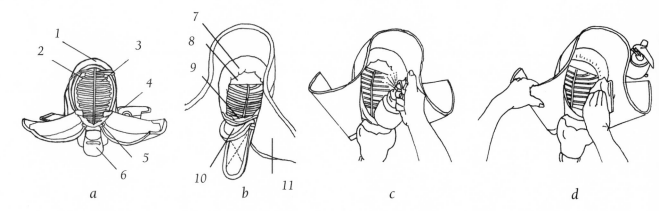

From the outset, a student must know how to care for and repair his kendo equipment. Figures 4.2*a* and *b* show the various parts of the men: (1) *buton*; (2) *ten*; (3) *chi*; (4) *mendare*; (5) *agodare*; (6) *tukidare*; (7) *uchiwa*; (8) *ten*; (9) *chi*; (10) *nijo ago*; and (11) *mendare*. Not shown is the center bar of the men, called the *talegane*. Figures 4.2*c* and *d* show how to clean the inside of your *men* with a water-filled atomizer and a dry cloth; this should be done at least monthly, and even more frequently if it is used quite often or if the humidity level is high. As figures 4.2*e* and *f* indicate, it is important to clean between the *uchiwa* and the *mendare* and always make sure that the *tukidare* is in line with the center of the *chi*. Figure 4.2*g* shows the correct way to return a wet *uchiwa* to its original form; figure 4.2*h* shows the incorrect way.

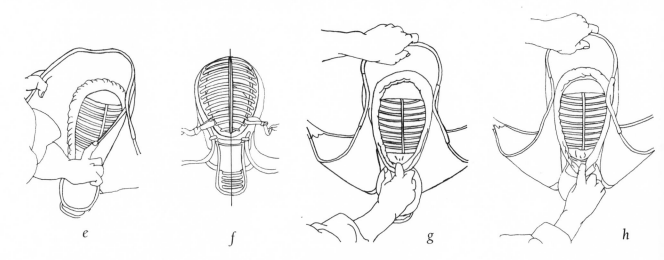

FIGURE 4.2. *The men.*

There are two ways the *menhimo*, or *men* strings, can be tied to hold the *men* in place on the head. Figure 4.3*a* shows a style of tying usually found in the Tokyo area; the *men* strings are tied from the bottom with the two *menchikawa*, one on each side tied to the fourth metal rung. The other method, usually found in the Osaka area and not illustrated here, involves only one *menchikawa* at the top of the *ten*, which is passed through the *menhimo* under the *chi* and then tied in back of the head. To store the *men* in a proper fashion, first pull the *mendare* straight down and bring them together, as shown in figure 4.3*b*. Now fold them up straight to the sides of the *men* and tie them in place with the *menhimo*, as demonstrated in figure 4.3*c*. Figure 4.3*d* shows a common but incorrect way to tie the *men*, one that keeps the back of the *mendare* off your neck and pushed forward.

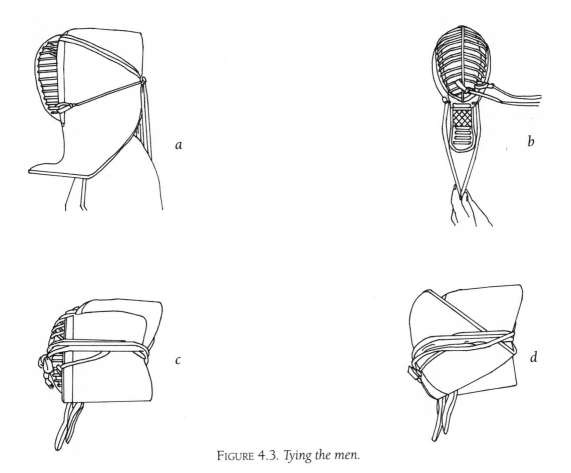

FIGURE 4.3. *Tying the men.*

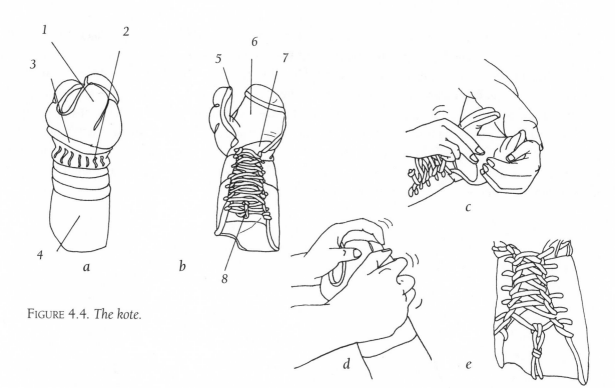

FIGURE 4.4. *The kote.*

The *kote* has eight parts (figs. 4.4*a* and *b*): (1) *koromo*, also called *kote gashira* or *nigira*; (2) *tsutsu*; (3) *kera*; (4) *kote hiji* or *tutubu*; (5) *kote ben*; (6) *uchigawa* or *te-no-uchigawa*; (7) *urako*; and (8) *kotehimo*.

The proper way to remove your *kote* is by grabbing the back and pulling forward (fig. 4.5*a*). The left *kote* should always be taken off and put on first. Improper removal of the *kote* can pull it apart at the stitching (fig. 4.5*b*).

FIGURE 4.5 (*a–b*). *Removal and care of the kote.*

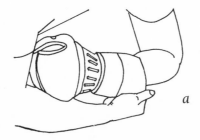

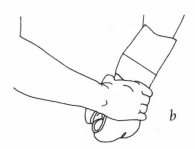

After the *kote* is removed, the palm of the glove should be straightened, using gentle pulls with the thumb and forefinger (figs. 4.4*c* and *d*). The *kote* should also be re-formed to its original shape (figs. 4.5*c* and *d*). Inasmuch as the *kote* is likely to be wet, tugging too hard on it can damage the *uchigawa* where it connects to the *koteben*. Figure 4.4*e* shows the proper lacing of the *kote* and the *kotehimo* (the knot).

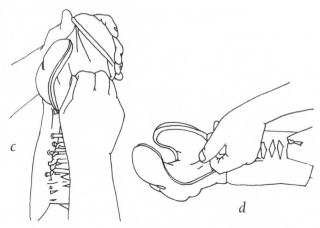

FIGURE 4.5 (*c-d*). *Removal and care of the kote.*

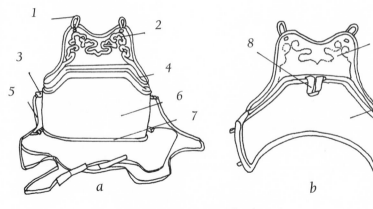

FIGURE 4.6. *The do.*

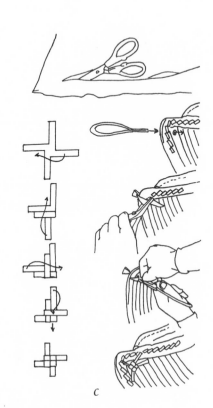

The *do* has ten parts (figs. 4.6*a* and *b*): (1) *munechikawa*; (2) *muneate*, also called *domune*; (3) *dochikawa*; (4) *komune* or *mochidashi*; (5) *dohimo*; (6) *dokawa*; (7) *hengana*; (8) *wa*; (9) *uchimune*; and (10) *do*. The *do* can be formed with from forty-three to seventy bamboo strips, which are painted a vivid reddish or orange color and then covered with rawhide coated with Japanese lacquer. Figure 4.6*c* demonstrates the repairing of the top or bottom of the *dochikawa* where the *dohimo* is attached to the body of the *do*. It is helpful to use the broken leather as a pattern for the new piece.

At the completion of practice, always wipe the outside of the *do* clean with a damp cloth (fig. 4.7*a*). About once a month, I use a leather protector, such as Armor-All, on the leather and brush the *domune* with a firm but not harsh hairbrush (fig. 4.7*b*). For the intricate brocade work, you can use an old toothbrush (see fig. 4.7*c*). The *tare*, or hip protectors (figs. 4.7*d* and *e*), comprise five elements: (1) *tareobi*; (2) *oodare*; (3) *kodare*; (4) *oodare*; and (5) *tarehimo*. The three *oodare* are the large outside protectors; the center one is where the name of the kendoist is displayed on the *tare* name cover. The *kodare* is the small or inside protector; the *tarehimo*, also called the tying *obi*, are on the right and left side. One proper way to put on the *tarehimo*, shown in figure 4.7*e*, is to roll the ties so as to keep the material straight and new looking. After rolling them in a small roll you can place a rubber band around them, or once the ties are straight, you can unroll them and place them around the side *oodare*, folding the ends under the bands you have made.

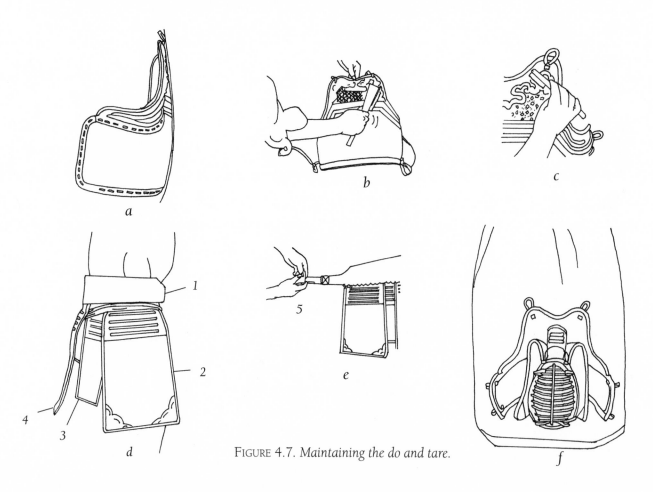

FIGURE 4.7. *Maintaining the do and tare.*

There are specific ways to tie bows and knots in your kendo equipment. Figures 4.8*a–g* show one way to tie the *hakama obi*. Figures 4.8*h* and i show variations of the same tie, achieved by tucking in the top part of the bow to the rear of the knot. Figures 4.8*j–m* show the *hakama's* proper *obi* tie. I show how to fold the *hakama* properly in my book *Iai: The Art of Drawing the Sword.**

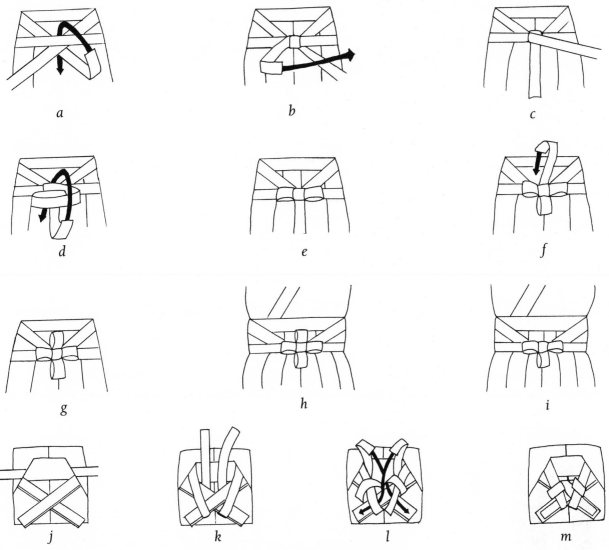

FIGURE 4.8. *Tying the hakama obi.*

*Darrell Max Craig, *Iai: The Art of Drawing the Sword* (Rutland, Vt.: Tuttle, 1988).

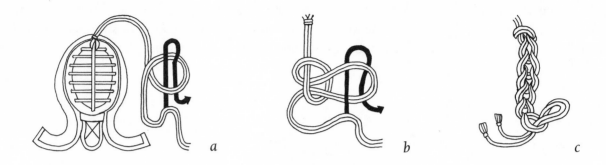

Figures 4.9*a–c* illustrate an easy way to tie the *menhimo* that keeps the strings straight and out of the way. Figures 4.9*d–h* show still another way to tie the *hakama obi*.

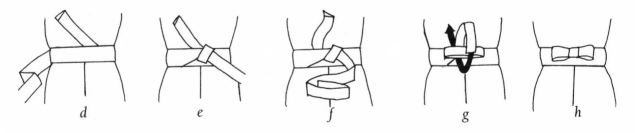

FIGURE 4.9. *Tying the menhimo (a–c) and hakama obi (alternative method) (d–h).*

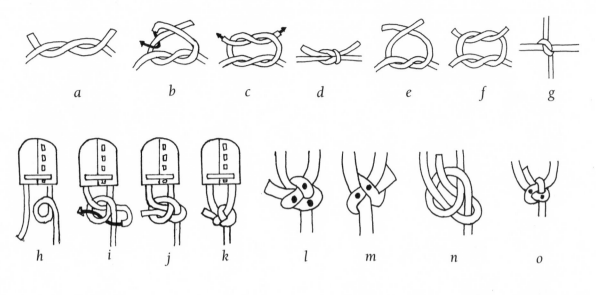

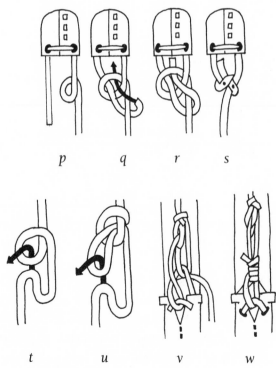

Figures 4.10a–g illustrate how to splice a broken *tsuri*. This should only be a temporary repair; a new one should be put on the *shinai* as soon as possible. Figures 4.10 a–d are correct; figures 4.10e–g shows another possible method, but it is incorrect. Figures 4.10h–s show two correct ways to tie the *tsuru* to the *sakigawa*. Figures 4.10t–w demonstrate tying the *tsuru* to the *tsuka*. Chiba Sensei once told me that the *tsuru* was originally taken from the Japanese musical instrument called the koto.

FIGURE 4.10. *Splicing a broken tsuri and tying the tsuru.*

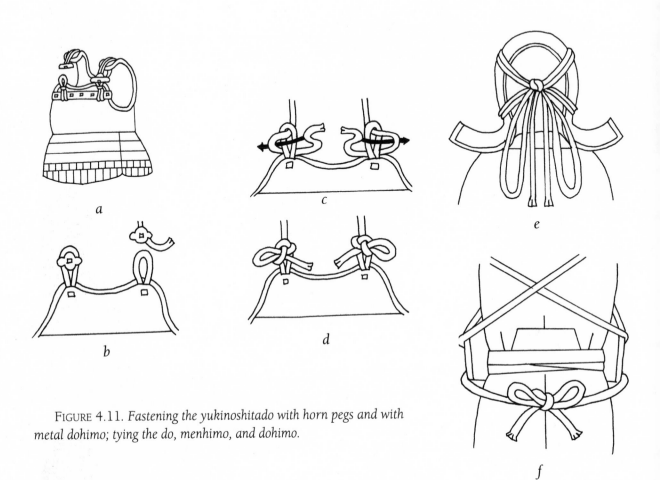

FIGURE 4.11. *Fastening the yukinoshitado with horn pegs and with metal dohimo; tying the do, menhimo, and dohimo.*

Figure 4.11*a* shows the *yukinoshitado* with the tying strings and the horn pegs. If you use a metal *dohimo* to fit in the *munechikawa*, its metal piece replaces the horn peg as in figure 4.11*b*. Most Japanese *sensei* frown upon the use of metal clips; I don't know why. I used a Japanese coin with a hole in the center to tie my do, until I tired of being told I should tie it as shown in figures 4.11*c* and *d*. When you tie the bow in the rear of the *men*, you should pull all the *menhimo* strings until they are straight and even, as in figure 4.11*e*. When tying the *dohimo,* make sure the bow is even, the bow loops are pointing up, and the bow ends are pointing down, as in figure 4.11*f*.

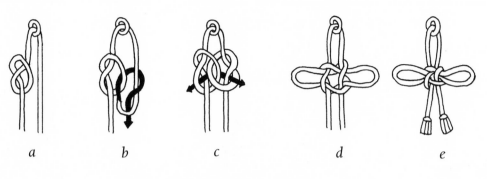

a   *b*   *c*   *d*   *e*

FIGURE 4.12 (*a–f*). *Tying the kaduto*

Figures 4.12*a–f* show how to tie the *kaduto*. Figures 4.12*g–k* show a simple way to tie *nishijin* or *jindachi* (the sword bags). Figures 4.12*l–r* show a more complicated way, which is similar to the *kaduto* knot.

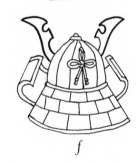

f

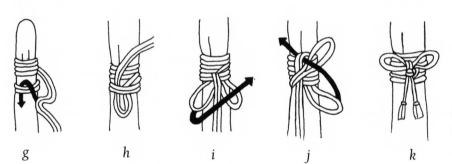

g   *h*   *i*   *j*   *k*

FIGURE 4.12 (*g–k*) . *Tying the nishijin (simple method).*

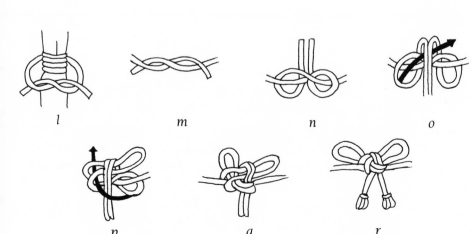

l   *m*   *n*   *o*

FIGURE 4.12 (*l–r*). *Tying the nishijin (alternative method).*

p   *q*   *r*

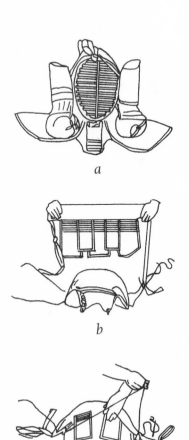

a

b

c

A proper way to store the kendo equipment in the *bogu* bag is demonstrated in figure 4.7*f*. If you do not use a *bogu* bag and wish to hang your *bogu* to dry, then the following steps are necessary. First, take the *menhimo*, place them through the *kote*, and tie them together through the *ten* (fig. 4.13*a*). Then place the *do*, with the top away from you, and the *tare* on top of the *do*, with the *tare obi* facing you (fig. 4.13*b*). Now bring the large *dohimo* on each side of the *do* across the back side of the *tare*, cross them in the middle, and tie them on the inside of the *do* (fig. 4.13*c*). Then roll the *tarehimo*, fasten them with a rubber band, and place the *men* and *kote* inside the *do*. Then take the remaining *men* strings and place them through the *munechikawa* and tie them together, leaving a loop by which to hang the *bogu* (fig. 4.13*d*). You can also use the *do* to hang the *bogu*.

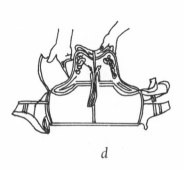

d

FIGURE 4.13. *Preparing the bogu for storage.*

The *shinai* comes in sizes ranging from 32 inches for children to 39 inches for adults. In this book I discuss only the 38-inch and 39-inch *shinai*, which, in general, weigh from 470 to 570 grams. You can buy them complete with the items listed in figure 4.14*a*, or just the bamboo itself, as in figure 4.14*b*; more experienced kendoists usually prefer the latter. Tournament *shinai* must weigh in at least 500 grams to be eligible for use by *men* and 470 grams for use by women. There is also the set of *nito shinai* used in the two-swords style called *nito ryu*, of which the small *shinai* weights 450 grams and the large *shinai* 550 grams.

The nine components of the *shinai* are as follows (fig. 4.14*a*): (1) the bamboo shaft (including the *omote*, or face, on the left and the *ura*, or rear, on the right), which should always be straight and not as in figure 4.14*c*; (2) *chigiri*, the metal square; (3) *tsuka-gashira*, the handle, for which there are four levels of quality; (4) *tsukadome*, which is made of rubber or leather; (5) *tsuba*, the guard made of leather or plastic; (6) *tsura*, the *shinai* string, which is white, yellow, red, or purple; (7) *nakayui*, made in two qualities of leather; (8) *sakigomu*, which is made of rubber and comes in sizes of 5, 8, 9, and 11 mm.; and (9) *sakigawa*, made in leather of two qualities. Figure 4.14*d* shows a special tool called the *shinai-kezuri*, which is used for repairing splintered *shinai* bamboo. There is also a special *shinai* bamboo oil, but a good quality 3:1 oil works just as well.

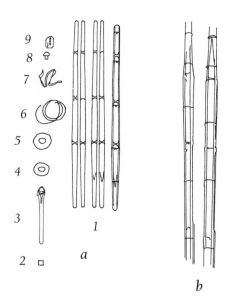

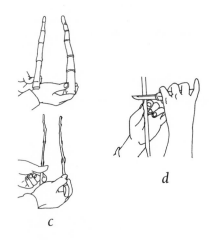

FIGURE 4.14. *The shinai and shinai-kezuri.*

The type, approximate cost, length, and weight of various *shinai* are shown in table 4.1. Prices vary depending upon the quality of the bamboo and whether the *shinai* are handmade. (Prices are by mail order from Japan—these items are extremely difficult to obtain in the U.S.—and will also fluctuate with the dollar/yen exchange rate.)

TABLE 4.1. SHINAI

Type	Approx. cost	Length	Weight
Kiyomasa	$20–27	38"	470 grams
Tozan	$24–35	38" 39"	530 grams 570 grams
Zenfu	$35–45	38" 39"	530 grams 570 grams
Kyoto-eizan	$45–50	38" 39"	530 grams 530 grams
Zen	$48–55	38" 39"	530 grams 530 grams
Tenryu	$85	39"	500 grams
Chikuho	$90	39"	520 grams
Carbon *shinai*	$195–225	38" 39"	530 grams 570 grams
Carbon *shinai* (Oval grip)	$265–325	38" 39"	530 grams 570 grams

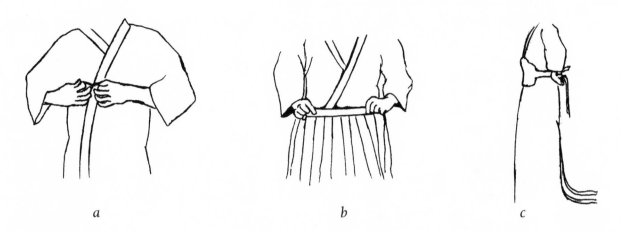

a   b   c

The *keiko-gi* consists of the top, called the *uwagi*, and the bottom, called the *hakama*. The *uwagi* is either white or indigo blue; children wear a white or a blue-checkered *uwagi* until the age of thirteen. Figure 4.15*a* shows the proper way to tie the *uwagi*. Tie first the inside strings and then the outside strings. Once the *uwagi* is in place, take the *hakama* by the front and step into the two large legs (fig. 4.15*b*). Drop the back of the *hakama* and take hold of the two long tie strings, bring them around to your backside, cross them and bring them around to the front again, cross them, and then once more take them to your backside (fig. 4.15*c*). At that point, tie them in a bow (fig. 4.15*d*). Be sure that the tie strings have stayed straight and flat while bringing them back and forth (fig. 4.15*e*). Now pick up the back of the *hakama* and place the back hard plate over the tied bow you made with the front ties. Bring the back tie strings to the front. Tie them in a square knot and tuck the ends in at your sides and to the rear (fig. 4.16*a*).

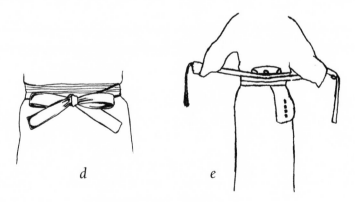

d   e

FIGURE 4.15. Tying the uwagi.

Japanese court dress. On the left is the kataginu with naga bakana, worn in high court. The hakama was sewn shut at the bottom and extended three to four feet behind the heels. This was to restrict any quick movements. A samurai could swing the excess train with his hands from left to right and, kneeling, walk with surprising rapidity. This was called "samurai walking." On the right is the gokenin, worn outside the inner chambers of the castle by hatamoto and lower-ranking samurai. Samurai below the rank of hatamoto could not wear the naga bakana.

THE NAMES AND SIGNIFICANCE OF
THE HAKAMA PLEATS

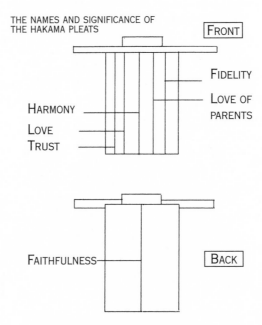

FRONT

FIDELITY

LOVE OF PARENTS

HARMONY

LOVE

TRUST

FAITHFULNESS

BACK

The hakama, or skirtlike trousers that are part of traditional Japanese dress. For the samurai, each of the six pleats of the hakama has symbolic significance.

Figure 4.16 illustrates how to put on the *bogu*. You should always be in *seiza* when putting on your kendo armor. First, take your *tare* and place it around your hips by bringing the tie strings around your body and tying them in front under the middle *oodare* in a bow (figs. 4.16*b* and *c*). Be sure that the *tare* tie strings are straight in the back and are not wrinkled or crossed (fig. 4.16*d*). Then place the *do* over the front of your *tare* by bringing the top *dohimo* to your rear, first over your right shoulder and then over your left. Then tie them into the *munechikawa*. Now bring the bottom *dohimo* to your rear and tie them together in a bow (fig 4.16*e*).

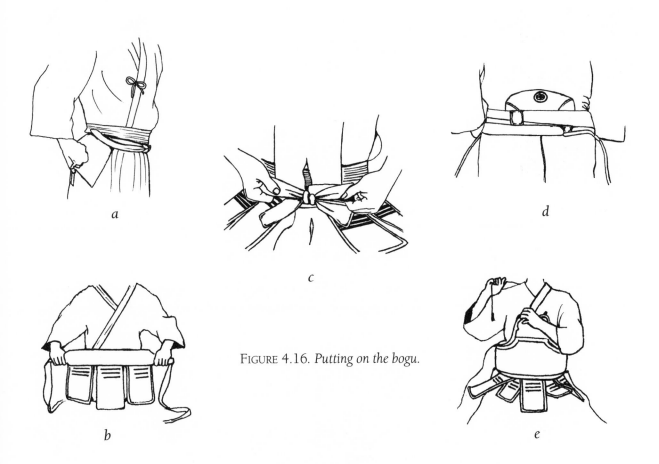

FIGURE 4.16. *Putting on the bogu.*

FIGURE 4.17 (a–f). *Two ways of folding the tenugui.*

Next, put on your tenugui, which is the head towel. First, place the towel to the rear of your head, take hold of the bottom of each end, let it fold forward, and bring the ends to your front (see figs. 4.17*a* and *b*). Then wrap the right side around to your left side and the left side to your right by tucking the ends at the bottom just behind your ears (fig. 4.17*c*). Fold the pointed end under and pull your ears out from under the *tenugui* (figs. 4.17*d* and *e*). You are now ready to put on your *men*. My dojo was once visited by Haga Sensei, who showed us a simple way of folding the *tenugui*, illustrated in figure 4.17*g*.

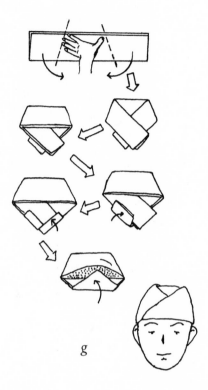

g

FIGURE 4.17 (g). *Two ways of folding the tenugui.*

To put on the *men,* place your chin on the *chi* and slide it backward on your head. Now bring the *menhimo* to the back of your head and cross them forward again, placing the ends through the top of the *ten* (fig. 4.17*f*). Now pull the strings tightly and bring them to the back of your head again, and then around and on top of your *tukidare.* Finally, bring them back to the rear of your head and tie them together in a bow (fig. 4.18*a*). The ends of all of the strings should be even.

It is now time to put on your *kote*. As I stated above, the left *kote* is put on first and taken off first (fig. 4.18*b*). Accordingly, put on the *kote* by the *tutubu*. You are now ready for *keiko*.

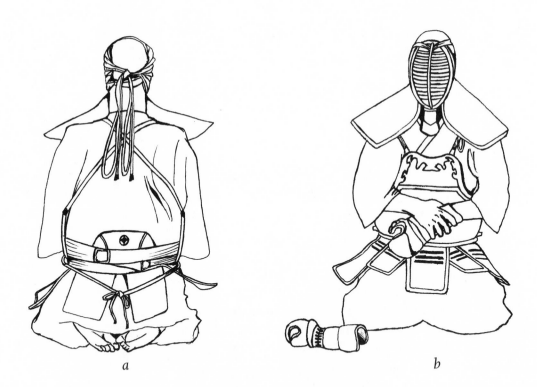

a   *b*

FIGURE 4.18. *Putting on the men and kote.*

5
KEIKO

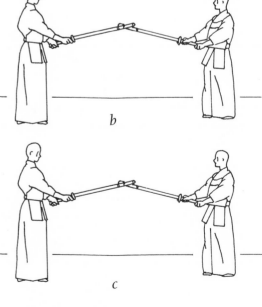

THIS chapter addresses some of the features of a typical kendo practice session.

MAAI, SONKYU, BREATHING, AND FOOT PLACEMENT

Maai is a Japanese term that essentially means "distance" and, when used in the martial arts, refers to the correct distance between two opponents or practitioners. Correct *maai* is critical in any martial art. If you are too close to your opponent, you will find it difficult to avoid his attack; if you are too far away, you will find it difficult to execute your own attack. Figure 5.1 illustrates three different types of *maai* in the context of kendo. *Toi-maai* (fig. 5.1*a*) is the distant interval. *Issoku-itto-no-maai* (fig. 5.1*b*), known as the one-sword or one-step interval, is an excellent one when practicing. It allows you to take a half-step forward, cross swords, and still see what action your opponent will take. If he steps backward, you follow quickly with one full step forward and launch your attack. If he steps forward, you should be in cutting distance. If you are closer than this one-

FIGURE 5.1. *Three types of maai.*

A "war fan" (gunsen)—sometimes called an "iron fan" (tetsu-sen, or tessen)—that Harutane Chiba Sensei presented to me in the late 1980s. Sensei had written on the fan a famous saying by Miyamoto Musashi: "Under issoku-itto, distance is dangerous. You have to step forward, as it is safer."

step interval, you should already have begun to execute a *waza*, whether it be to the left, right, backward, or forward. *Chikai-maai* (fig. 5.1c) is the near interval. These three types are discussed in more detail in chapter 8 in the context of specific *kendo kata*.

Sonkyu is one of the most important postures in kendo and one of the most informative to the knowledgeable observer, to whom it can tell a great deal about the quality of your training, the strength of your kendo, and your probable weaknesses. *Sonkyu* starts by squatting and bending your knees outward approximately ninety degrees (see fig. 5.2a and b). Your head and back must be kept straight. Balance on the balls of your feet with your heels turned inward. Your *shinai* should be in the center of your body and the *sakigawa* should be pointing at your opponent's throat. Your arms are away from your body. *Sonkyu* must be taken each time your draw your *shinai* from your side, as

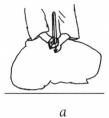

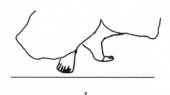

a   *b*

FIGURE 5.2 (*a–b*). *Sonkyu*.

when you start a kendo match or begin practice. Figure 5.2c shows both kendoists in *sonkyu*. In figure 5.2d they stand up and assume *toi-maai*, and in figure 5.2e they have advanced to *chikai-maai*. Figures 5.2f–h demonstrate how to rise from *sonkyu* when engaging in *kirikaeshi*, a cutting exercise discussed in detail later in this chapter. In figure 5.2f the kendoists have taken *sonkyu* in the *issoku-itto-no-maai*. As they stand, they maintain *issoku-itto-no-maai* and are now ready to start *kirikaeshi* (fig. 5.2g). Both kendoists, after viewing the opponent and determining where a weakness may exist, attack forward (fig. 5.2h).

Figure 5.2 (c–h). *Sonkyu.*

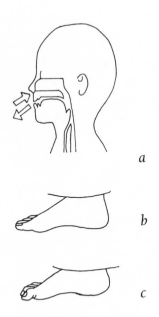

While practicing *waza* or *kirikaeshi*, your breathing pattern should be normal. Breathe in through your nose and out through your mouth as illustrated in figure 5.3*a*. Figure 5.3*b* shows correct placement of the right foot: the toes are pointing forward normally and the heel is barely off the floor, just far enough to slide a piece of paper under it. Figure 5.3*c* shows incorrect foot placement: although the heel is correct, the toes are tight; they are gripping the floor. This tightening of the toe and leg muscles will result in abnormal leg movement. The left foot, which is in the rear, will be positioned the same as in figure 5.2*b* except that the heel will be a little higher off the floor. This is discussed in more depth in chapter 8 in the context of specific *kata*.

FIGURE 5.3.
*Proper breathing and
foot position.*

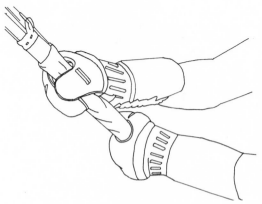

PROPER GRIP ON THE TSUKA

It is important to hold the *tsuka* correctly when performing any cutting motion with the *shinai* (fig. 5.4). The right hand—which is on top—is merely the guide to the target, whereas the left hand actually performs the cutting. To perform a correct cutting action, whether *men*, *kote*, *do*, or *tsuki*, the right hand rotates inward with the thumb pointing down while the left does the same. Most *sensei* describe this movement as wringing out a wet towel. Once the cut is complete, the right hand relaxes and becomes a guide once again.

FIGURE 5.4. *Holding the shinai.*

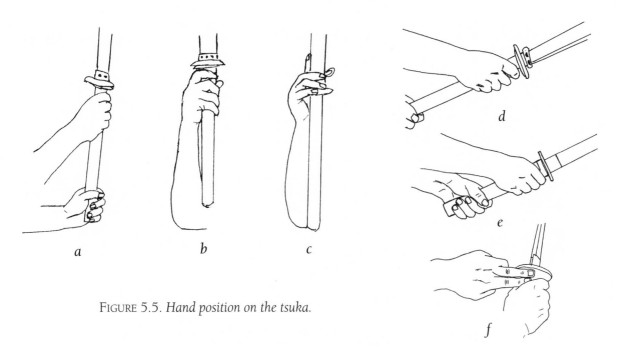

FIGURE 5.5. *Hand position on the tsuka.*

Figure 5.5*a* shows the proper distance between the hands when gripping the *tsuka*. The proper length for the *tsuka* depends on your arm length; that shown in figure 5.5*b* is correct, while that in figure 5.5*c* is too long. Measure the *tsuka* with the proper left-hand grip, as shown in figure 5.5*d*. The grip for the *katana* and the *shinai* are the same (see fig. 5.5*e*), even though the *tsuka* is longer on the *shinai*. Figure 5.5*f* demonstrates the proper distance between the *tsuba* and the right forefinger; this should be the same whether you are using a *shinai* or a *katana*.

No portion of the *tsuka* should extend behind the left hand. Figures 5.6*a* and *b* illustrate correct left-hand grips; Chiba Sensei told me that the first of these was the most common grip in the old days whether the samurai was using a *katana* or a *shinai*. Figures 5.6*c* and *d* illustrate incorrect grips on *shinai* and *katana*, respectively: an inch or so of *tsuka* extends beyond the little finger.

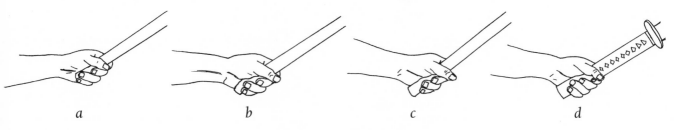

FIGURE 5.6. *The left-hand grip.*

Figure 5.7 illustrates proper hand positions from different angles. Note that the thumbs point down.

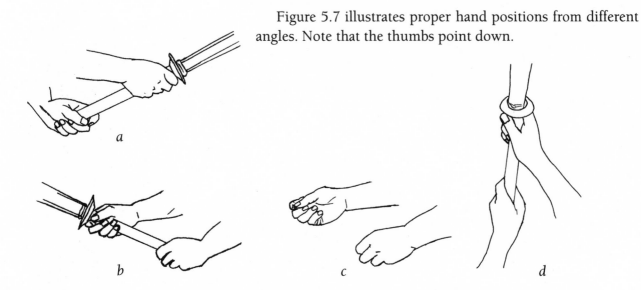

FIGURE 5.7. *The grip viewed from various angles.*

The similarity between grips for the *shinai* and the European fencing saber can be seen in figure 5.8. In both grips, the thumbs point down and the other fingers grip lightly. My maestro in French fencing once told me, "Hold the blade like a baby bird: tight enough so it cannot escape, but not so tight that you kill it." With the saber, however, the thumb and forefinger perform the proper cutting action, whereas with the *shinai* you use the last two fingers of the left hand (fig. 5.8*c* and *d*).

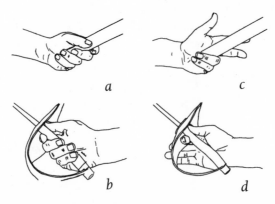

FIGURE 5.8. *Similarities between the shinai grip and the European fencing saber grip.*

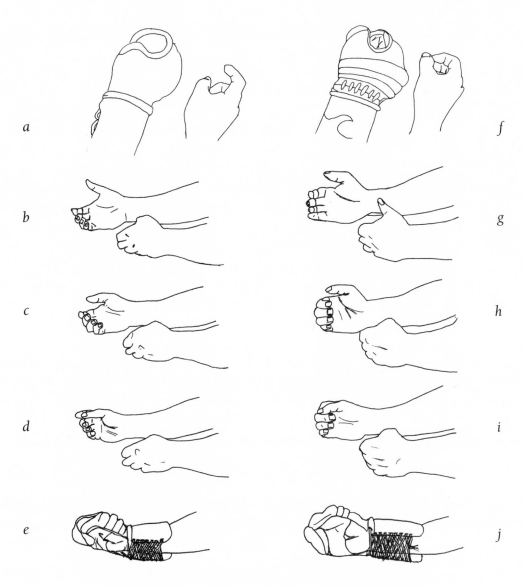

FIGURE 5.9. *Grips with the hakataya and the standard kote.*

A special *kote* made in Japan, called the *hakataya*, allows you to turn your thumbs down properly (fig. 5.9*a*); figures 5.9*b–e* show the grip used with the *hakataya*. The standard *kote* is shown in figure 5.9*f*, with its grip in figures 5.9*g–j*.

THE BASIC STANCE

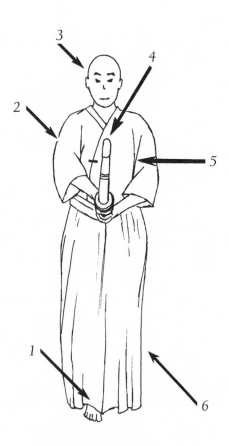

FIGURE 5.10. *The basic stance.*

Figure 5.10 illustrates six basic points to keep in mind whethe you are a beginner or an advanced student:

1. *Ashi* (foot or feet). Make sure that your feet are correctly positioned one fist apart, toes pointing forward. Both heels should be off the floor. The right (front) hee should be off the floor enough to slide a piece of pape under it; the left (rear) heel should be off the floor abou a quarter of an inch. The ball of the left foot should be i line with the right heel.
2. *Hiji* (elbows). The elbows should be away from the body and forward so that the arms form somewhat of a circle Keep the arms and elbows natural.
3. *Metsuke* (to look; eyes; focus). Look at your opponent eyes as if you were looking at a picture on a wall: the op ponent's eyes are the picture, his body is the frame and wall. If your opponent has an improper stance, or if h moves his sword in some odd way and creates an open ing, you will see the opening just as if the picture ha suddenly tilted.
4. *Kensen* (sword tip). The sword tip must point at your op ponent's throat at all times and be kept in the center o your body. Your thumbs must point down, always keep ing in mind that the right hand is merely the guide fo the cut and the left hand actually cuts.
5. *Hij* (armpits). Keep your armpits open by pushing you elbows forward and slightly outward from your body.
6. *Hiza* (knees). Your knees should always be bent slightl) If you raise the left (rear) heel excessively, the left kne will be bent too much. You must be able to push off wit the left foot in a natural manner.

Figure 5.11 shows six important check points for prope center posture while holding the *shinai*.

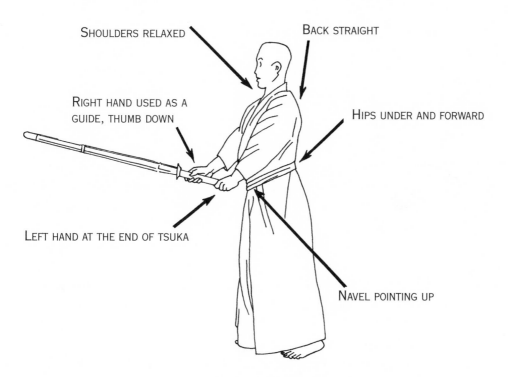

FIGURE 5.11. *The basic stance: side view.*

SHOULDERS RELAXED

BACK STRAIGHT

RIGHT HAND USED AS A
GUIDE, THUMB DOWN

HIPS UNDER AND FORWARD

LEFT HAND AT THE END OF TSUKA

NAVEL POINTING UP

JOGE-BURI

One of the most fundamental exercises in kendo is *joge-buri*, involving vertical swings of the *shinai*. When you begin to swing the *shinai* up and over your head, push outward and upward with your left hand, keeping your arms extended and your elbows bent slightly outward so that they pass by your ears in a normal manner. Figure 5.12*a* demonstrates the correct way to initiate the movement. In figure 5.12*b*, the incorrect way, the kendoist has begun by pulling with the right hand, which may seem faster but is one of the most common mistakes a kendoist makes. When you pull inward toward your body with the right hand, you expose your *kote* and create a direct path to your *men*. If you pull even slightly toward your body with your right hand, it becomes almost impossible to protect the *kote*.

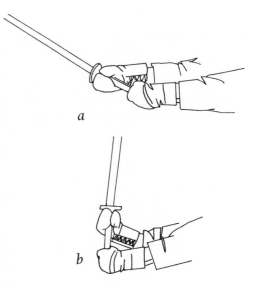

a

b

FIGURE 5.12 (*a–b*). *Joge-buri.*

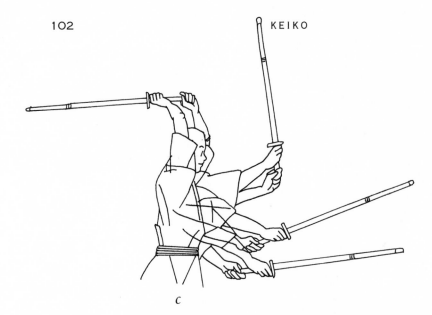

FIGURE 5.12 (c). *Joge-buri.*

Swinging the *shinai* vertically and diagonally may seem simple, but it is one of the most difficult things to accomplish correctly. As you begin the exercise, keep in mind that, at the end of the cut, your hand should perform the "wringing of the towel" motion discussed earlier. The *shinai* must travel on an imaginary line corresponding to the center of your body. It travels up that line above your head and moves down the same line to your front (fig. 5.12*c*). When beginning to learn this exercise, you might want to practice it in front of a mirror and without moving your feet. As you become more experienced, you can add the front and back footwork that accompanies each swing of the *shinai*. That is, as you swing the *shinai* up, you will step back with your left foot and then your right. As you swing the *shinai* down, you will slide your right foot forward followed by your left, always bending your knees slightly as you move and swing the *shinai*.

Naname-buri is the act of downward swings of the *shinai* to the right and left. The angle of each downward swing must be the same. It starts the same as in *joge-buri* but, as the downward swing starts from the center of your forehead, the *shinai* will travel on a twenty-degree angle on your right and on your left. Again, just before completion of the downward movement, be sure to squeeze and wring the *tsuka*. This exercise will help the student learn to cut correctly to the right and the left *men*. These two techniques of *joge-buri* and *naname-buri* require enormous amounts of practice. The *joge-buri* with footwork will eventually teach the student to perform *haya-suburi* correctly. *Haya-suburi*, sometimes called *chouyaku-suburi*, is a forward and backward jumping motion performed by pushing off with the rear foot when moving forward and pushing off with the front foot when going backward. The feet must remain in the same correct position at all times with only the balls of the feet touching the floor on each movement while the *shinai* moves on its center line back and forth.

WARM-UP EXERCISES

Kendo has unique exercises to warm up the body, develop good posture, and develop good movements with the *shinai*. Most of these exercises resemble actual cutting movements employed in *kenjitsu*. One such exercise, called *suburi* or *zenshinkotai*, is performed by striking the *shomen*, *kote*, *do*, and *tsuki*. To perform this exercise, imagine an opponent of approximately your own height facing you. Move forward with the right foot and then the left, strike, and retreat by moving the left foot and then the right.

At my dojo we usually do these exercises about ten times each, starting out solo, then proceeding with a partner where required. When we do them using the *uchikomi-bo* and *bogu*, we follow the same pattern in order to learn to follow through after the strike using *okuri-ashi* footwork (as described in chapter 8) and taking *zanshin*. We do the following pattern of strikes: *men*, *kote-men*, *kote-do*, *men-kote-do*, *men-tairtari-do*, *men-tairtari-do-kote-men*, and then *men-tairtari-do* followed by the *motodachi* (the holder of the *uchikomi-bo*) doing *debana-do* as the attacker finishes this exercise with a *shomen*. We call this series "*waza*

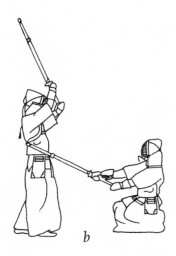

FIGURE 5.13. *Sonkyu-do.*

"1–7" and repeat it one, two, or three times, varying the strike points, such as *men*, *men* and *kote-men*, and so on.

A good exercise to practice before putting on your *men* is *sonkyu-do*, or as we call it, squat *do*. This *shomen-kaeshi-do* is performed by leaping forward five times and backward five times in the *sonkyu* (squatting) position while receiving *men* strikes from the *motodachi*. To start, the attacker takes *sonkyu*; the *motodachi* stands to his front, strikes at his *shomen*, then takes one step back. The attacker blocks the *men* cut with the *omote*, or left face, of the *shinai* (fig. 5.13*a*), a move referred to as *kaeshi-do*. Then the attacker leaps forward while executing a *kaeshi-do* to the *motodachi's* right side (fig. 5.13*b*). As the attacker leaps forward, it is important for both feet to strike the floor simultaneously with his execution of the *kaeshi-do*. The *motodachi* now steps back again and strikes at the attacker's *shomen* (fig. 5.13*c*). The attacker blocks again, this time using the *ura*, or right face, of the *shinai*, and leaps forward, striking the *motodachi's* left *do*. This exercise continues until the attacker moves forward five times. The *motodachi* then steps forward and strikes at the attacker's *shomen*. The attacker now leaps backward to block and strike the *motodachi's do*. Whether moving forward or backward, the attacker must keep in rhythm with the *motodachi's* attacks. He must also maintain his balance and correct *maai* at all times. This exercise, which can be done with the *men* on or off, builds timing, balance, and posture and—most important—strengthens the legs.

These basic movements in *uchikomi* training are the basis for all sword strikes and thrusts used in kendo. It is most important to practice these fundamental movements of striking *men*, *kote*, *do*, and *tsuki* in *uchikomi*—that is, without actually striking. (In fact, *uchikomi* means "to strike the air," striking an imaginary opponent, though sometimes one practices with a partner as a target to strike toward.) When practicing *uchikomi*, strive to combine eye, hand, and foot movements. This will enable you to start to understand the basic kendo techniques and to develop these basic moves and skills to a point when you can use them freely and in any combination. You must develop your knowledge of basics until you reach a level where you can activate the element of thought that is inherent in the Japanese word *keiko.*

Chiba Sensei's father had a way of describing this process of learning the fundamentals. The true Japanese swordsman, he said, has to go through three stages, called *shu, ha,* and *ri. Shu* is the time that the *sensei* of the dojo has to protect the student, not only from outside elements but also from himself, and this stage is symbolically an egg. The student, like the chick inside the egg, is developing form and technique. This first stage is hard, and the form or shape of each technique must be protected and mastered. The egg's hard shell symbolizes the fundamental beginning. The second stage, *ha,* or breaking form, is when the chick inside the egg breaks out. The student in this secondary stage starts to learn the application of the basic fundamentals, or *bunkai,* to each movement. The fundamentals are mastered and can be applied in any situation. In the third and final stage, *ri,* the student, like the chick, has fully matured and is ready to leave the nest. The student now can apply his techniques subconsciously and must leave bad habits and old ideas behind him. His training has fully matured. The student must now seek out what the master of the dojo cannot teach him, perfection of the protection that lies in each technique.

KIRIKAESHI

Kirikaeshi, a basic exercise for learning to strike or cut the *shomen* and the left and right *yokomen* (the center and sides of the head, respectively), is also called *uchikaeshi,* or consecutive left and right head strikes. It should always begin and finish a

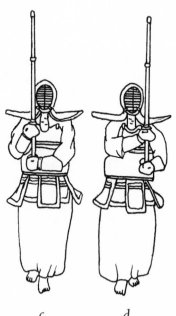

regular kendo practice. The exercise starts with the kendoist in the *chudan-no-kamae* (center sword posture) and in the *sonkyu* position. The attacker then stands, being sure his feet are pointing forward correctly (fig. 5.14*a*; fig. 5.14*b* is incorrect).

Figures 5.14*c* and *d* represent the *motodachi*, the kendoist who receives the strikes. It is the *motodachi*'s job to move back and forth five steps with each foot, using the *ayumi-ashi* method (described in chapter 8), while receiving his partner's cuts. The *motodachi* is not responsible for the correct *maai*; this is the responsibility of the attacker. Each strike to the *motodachi*'s *men* must be made with the first six to eight inches of the *shinai*.

FIGURE 5.14. *The kirikaeshi stance.*

FIGURE 5.15 (*a–c*). *The sequence of moves in kirikaeshi.*

The attacker begins *kirikaeshi* at the *issoku-itto-no-maai* or one-step sword interval (fig. 5.15*a*). The *motodachi* calls out "*kirikaeshi*" to his partner, and his partner replies by repeating the command, "*kirikaeshi*." The *motodachi* then lowers his *shinai* tip slightly to his right, allowing his *shomen* to be open for attack—or, alternatively, raises his *shinai* tip upward and to his right to expose his *men*. Either method is correct. The attacker now raises his *shinai* over his head (fig. 5.15*b*) and, while stepping forward with his right foot followed by his left, shouts "*Men!*" and strikes to the center of the *motodachi's men* (fig. 5.15*c*). When a novice attacker makes his first *men* strike, the *motodachi* usually does not move as he receives the strike. For the more advanced kendoist, the *motodachi* usually takes a half step back.

d

e

f

FIGURE 5.15 (d–f). *The sequence of moves in kirikaeshi.*

The attacker continues forward (figs. 5.15d and e). This point, when the opponents' *tsuba* and *tsuka* clash, is called *tsuba-zeriai*; if they both have armor on, it's called *taiatari* (body crashing). If you look ahead at figure 5.16a you will see that the strike is performed with the first six or eight inches of the *shinai* and the right arm is parallel with the floor. The left hand is turned inward, thumb pointing down. In figure 5.16b the *tsuka* are crossed and each *shinai* is about thirty degrees off center. The attacker's right foot is forward. At this point the *motodachi* steps back with his left foot, but his right foot does not move (fig. 5.16c). The attacker now steps backward, using *okuri-ashi* (described in chapter 8), until he is once again at an interval to strike *motodachi's men* with the first six to eight inches of his *shinai* (see fig. 5.15f).

Now look back at figures 5.14c and d to see how the *motodachi* receives the left and right strikes. The *motodachi* holds his *shinai* in a vertical position, with the left hand in the area where the *do* and *tare* come together and the right hand about even with his breast. Figure 5.14c shows him about to receive the right *yokomen* cut and figure 5.14d the left *yokomen* cut. The *motodachi* must not hold his hands too high when receiving the attacker's strikes.

The attacker starts his five *yokomen* strikes on the *motodachi's* left side. As the attacker makes his first side cut, the *motodachi* does not move and his right foot is forward (refer again to fig. 5.14d). Then, as the attacker advances forward with his right *yokomen,* the *motodachi* steps back with his right foot (fig. 5.14c). With each step, the *motodachi* moves his *shinai* from left to right and blocks each strike. The *motodachi* takes five steps back and then five steps forward. Again it is the attacker's job to maintain the correct *maai.*

g   h

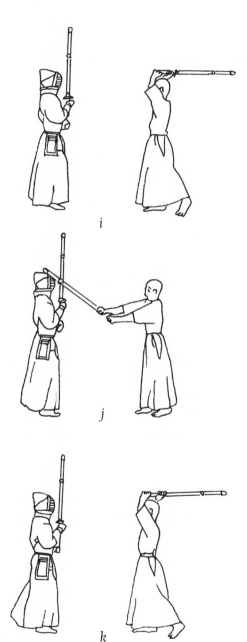

i

j

k

Each time he cuts the *motodachi*'s *men*, the attacker must make his strikes with large motions and the *shinai* placed well over his head (fig. 5.15*g*). Figure 5.15*h* illustrates the first left *yokomen*.

The attacker steps forward, with a large movement of the *shinai*, using *okuri-ashi* footwork (fig. 5.15*i*); the *motodachi* is as in figure 5.14*d* and steps back. The attacker then strikes the right *yokomen* (fig. 5.15*j*), while the motodachi is as in figure 5.14*c*. Note that as the attacker moves his *shinai* upward each time, as in figure 5.15*k*, the *motodachi* moves back.

FIGURE 5.15 (*g–k*). *The sequence of moves in kirikaeshi.*

The attacker now strikes the left *yokomen* (fig. 5.15*l*), steps forward again to strike (fig. 5.15*m*), and strikes the right *yokomen* (fig. 5.15*n*). Again he steps forward (fig. 5.15*o*) and strikes the left *yokomen* (fig. 5.15*p*).

At this point the attacker has advanced five steps forward. He now starts his five steps back while striking the motodachi's *yokomen*. The attacker is still responsible for keeping the correct *maai* and uses *okuri-ashi* footwork by moving his left (rear) foot back first. The fifth and final

FIGURE 5.15 (*l-p*). *The sequence of moves in kirikaeshi.*

q   r

yokomen strike going backward is on the left side of *motodachi*'s *men*. As the attacker makes his fifth and final strike, he assumes the *issoku-itto-no-maai* (fig. 5.15q).

The attacker now brings his *shinai* over his head (fig. 5.15r). The *motodachi* moves his *shinai* to the side, allowing his *men* to be open to receive the final *shomen-uchi* or center head strike (fig. 5.15s and t).

As soon as the attacker makes his final strike, the *motodachi* pivots on his right foot by moving his left foot to his right rear.

s   t

FIGURE 5.15 (*q–t*). *The sequence of moves in kirikaeshi.*

u   *v*

FIGURE 5.15 (*u–v*). *The sequence of moves in kirikaeshi.*

This allows the attacker to pass by him (fig. 5.15*u*). The attacker continues going forward using *okuri-ashi* footwork until he feels that, when he turns 180 degrees to his left, he will be at the *toi-maai* or distant interval (fig. 5.15*v*).

When performing *kirikaeshi* more than once, the second *shomen-uchi* (fig. 5.15*t*) becomes the opening *men* strike of the second *kirikaeshi*. In other words, the attacker would start again at figure 5.15*d*.

A few important things to remember about performing *kirikaeshi* are:

1. Each *yokomen* strike should be at an angle of about forty-five degrees.
2. All striking motions must be as large as possible.
3. Speed is not a factor; beginners must practice with slow and exaggerated movements.

a   *b*   *c*

FIGURE 5.16. *Tsuba-zeriai.*

4. The feet and hands must correctly accompany all body
   motions; in other words, when the hands and feet move,
   the *shinai* must also move. The back must be straight; do
   not bend at the waist. As a good training tool to keep the
   back straight, the beginner should squeeze the buttocks
   together when moving forward for the strike. After a
   while, he will be able to keep his back straight without the
   squeezing movement.
5. When making each cutting action, the *shinai* should swing
   up until it reaches a point well above the head.
6. Finish with a *shomen* or front center cut only after taking
   the correct *maai.*
7. Always start and end the *yokomen* strikes on the *motodachi's* left side.
8. Be sure the attacker's *kake-go* (shout) is carefully observed,
   so his breathing is in rhythm with his sharp *kiai* or yell.

Miscalculations in moving the shinai create openings for a men cut (top) and a deadly tsuki thrust (bottom).

HOW TO SEE OPENINGS IN KEIKO

Before we end this chapter, I want to discuss some common ways in which openings are created in kendo.

The unseen kendoist in figure 5.17a (the one with his back to you) has the *shinai* centered on his opponent, tip pointing at his throat. His right forward *kote* is turned inward correctly. He is in *chudan-no-kamae* and at *chikai-maai* (the near interval). He is controlling his opponent's *shinai* with the *omote* of his own *shinai* and is keeping the end of his *shinai* pointed at his opponent's throat. Remember: once the swords have crossed, only one kendoist can have true center.

Figure 5.17b illustrates how the *shinai* is moved up and down from the center of your opponent's chest to his throat. This action of the *shinai*'s *kensen* (tip) is performed by pushing down and lifting up slightly with the left hand. It can also be accomplished by pushing forward slightly with both hands. The arms are slightly away from your *do*. When you are engaged in this *chudan-no-kamae*, the *men* (point 1) is vulnerable in the up mode if you come off center just a little; the throat (point 2) becomes vulnerable on the down movement.

Figure 5.17c is the front view of figure 5.17b. As you can see, your opponent has come off center to his left trying to protect his *kote*. This automatically exposes his *men* (point 1) and his throat (point 2). Conversely, the kendoist in figure 5.17d has come off the center line to his right. This opens *men* (point 1), throat (point 2), and *kote* (point 3). In the photograph at the top of page 114, the kendoist on the right has pulled with his right hand as discussed previously and has created an opening for the *men* cut. In the bottom photograph the kendoist on the left has opened himself up for a deadly *tsuki* thrust.

The drawings in figures 5.17c and d exaggerate the *shinai*'s movements for purposes of illustration. In actuality it would be off center no more than its own thickness, as in figure 5.17a. The kendoist facing you in figure 5.17a is off center by only the

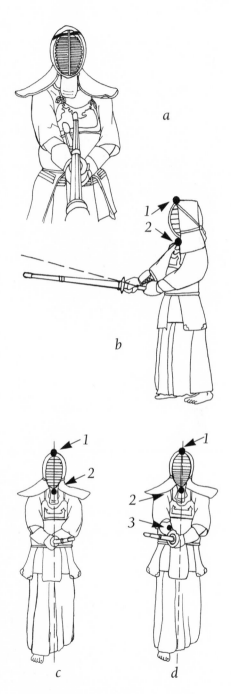

FIGURE 5.17. *Kendoists in chudan-no-kamae and at chikai-maai.*

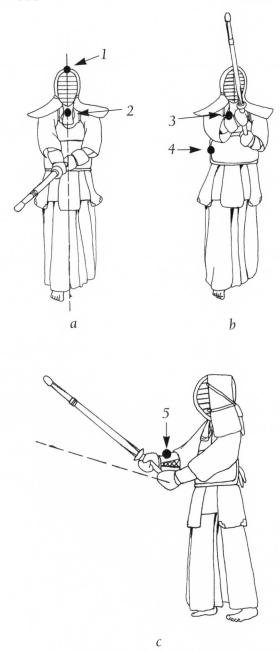

a

b

c

FIGURE 5.18. *Faulty positions of the shinai.*

thickness of his *shinai* and is vulnerable for a *tsuki* or *men* cut.

The kendoist in figure 5.18*a* has dropped his *shinai* down and off center to his right. This movement protects his *do* but unfortunately exposes his *men* (point 1) and throat (point 2). This happens when trying to protect the right side of the *do*. Students frequently make this mistake when thinking too much and trying to outguess what their attacker is going to do, instead of seeing and feeling his movement.

When you bring your *shinai* up too high and off center, as in figure 5.18*b*, perhaps to protect your *shomen* and *hidari-men*, the *kote* (point 3) and *migido* (point 4) become vulnerable. In the bottom photograph on page 114, the kendoist has not only brought his *shinai* up too high to protect his *men* but also stayed in that position so long that his opponent was able to attack his throat with *tsuki*.

The kendoist in figure 5.18*c* has kept the center line but has pulled with his right hand and moved the *shinai's kensen* above his opponent's head, thereby making his *kote* (point 5) open for attack.

The errors shown in figures 5.17 and 5.18 are only the most common mistakes that can lead a kendoist to expose an area for attack. A new kendo student, as a result of insufficient training, usually makes far too large a motion with the *shinai* to protect his *kote, men, tsuki,* or *do.* In this respect, as in all others, nothing can take the place of a good instructor.

6

BASIC UCHI

MEN, KOTE, DO

THIS chapter presents several *waza* for the basic *uchi* (strikes or cuts) of *men*, *kote*, and *do*, repetition of which will develop good mental and physical discipline. Practice these *waza* making slow and large movements with your *shinai*. Do not allow ego and premature speed to enter into your training. Bad habits learned at the beginning of training become almost impossible to break later.

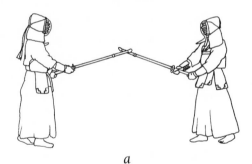

a

SHOMEN-UCHI

Shomen-uchi, the cut to the center of the head, starts in *issoku-itto-no-maai* and *chudan-no-kamae*, as demonstrated in figure 6.1a and described in detail in chapter 8; the *motodachi* is on the left. The *motodachi* moves his body slightly forward and his *kensen* slightly up. The attacker steps with his right foot and starts his attack (fig 6.1b).

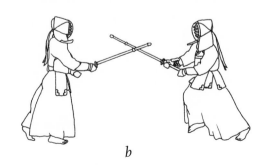

b

FIGURE 6.1 (*a–b*). *Shomen-uchi.*

c

d

e

FIGURE 6.1(*c–e*). *Shomen-uchi.*

The *motodachi* raises his *shinai* a little more and slightly to his left (fig. 6.1*c*). The attacker now brings his *shinai* over his head by pushing his left (rear) hand forward and strikes the *motodachi's men* (fig. 6.1*d*). The attacker follows through by bringing the left (rear) foot up quickly using *okuri-ashi* (described in chapter 8), going by the *motodachi* on his left side (fig. 6.1*e*).

This basic *men* strike can also be extended to more advanced techniques such as *men debana men* (described below) or *men debana kote*.

In executing *shomen-uchi*, do not break the movement of the *shinai* while swinging it up and then down. The first six to eight inches of the *shinai* are used to complete the cut. Do not spread your elbows too far, tense your shoulders, bend forward at the waist, or lift your front foot too far off the floor. Keep your body squarely toward the *motodachi* and both hands in the center line of your body.

FIGURE 6.2. *Kote-uchi.*

KOTE-UCHI

Kote-uchi also starts in *issoku-itto-no-maai* and *chudan-no-kamae*, as in figure 6.2*a*; again, the *moto-dachi* is on the left. The action starts with the attacker taking a small step forward on his right foot, followed by his left (fig. 6.2*b*). The *motodachi* reacts by stepping slightly forward and bringing the tip of his *shinai* up slightly to protect his *men* (fig. 6.2*c*). The attacker now swings his *shinai* up so his left hand is about even with his forehead or to a point where he can just see under his *tsuka* and hands. In figure 6.2*c* the attacker has already done this and is now bringing his *shinai* down. At the moment the attacker's right foot touches the floor on his forward movement, he simultaneously cuts the *motodachi's kote* (fig. 6.2*d*), making sure to bring the left (rear) foot up quickly using *okuri-ashi*. (All these basic moves use the *okuri-ashi*.)

The cut must be made with the whole body while moving forward, regardless of how small the move is; never use just the arms to complete this or any other cut. Bringing your left foot forward quickly will help you avoid bending at the hips. Note that this *waza* involves a cut to the *motodachi's* right (forward) *kote*; when cutting the left *kote*, the *motodachi* has to have his *shinai* above his head as in *jodan-no-kamae*, a position described in chapter 8.

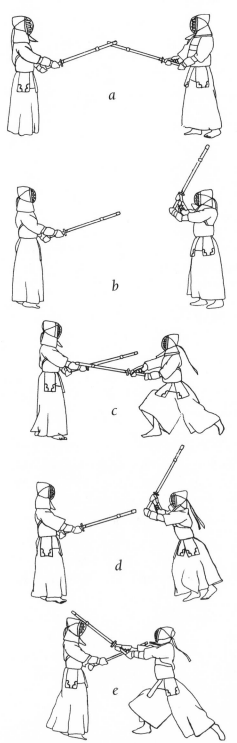

NIDAN-WAZA

The term *nidan-waza* applies to any combination of techniques consisting of two consecutive strikes and thrusts made in a single continuous motion. The *waza* described here combines strikes to the *kote* and *men*. In any *waza* involving multiple attacks, your first attack subconsciously exposes an area for your subsequent attack. Thus, as you attack the *kote* and then the *men*, remember that the strikes must be performed in an unbroken sequence.

Once again, the kendoists begin in *issoku-itto-no-maai* and *chudan-no-kamae*, as in figure 6.3a, with the *motodachi* on the left. The *waza* starts with the *motodachi* stepping slightly forward with his right foot. The attacker slides forward an inch or two, keeping *chudan-no-kamae*. The attacker's *shinai* should be pointed at the *motodachi*'s throat. The *motodachi* now moves his *shinai* off center and slightly to his left. The attacker, seeing the opening to the *motodachi*'s *kote*, steps forward with his front foot while bringing his *shinai* up as in the last *waza* (fig. 6.3b). The attacker now cuts the *motodachi*'s *kote* (fig. 6.3c), quickly brings his left foot forward while simultaneously swinging his *shinai* up again (fig. 6.3d), and cuts the *motodachi*'s *men* (fig. 6.3e). After the attacker has cut the *motodachi*'s *men*, he continues through on the right side of the *motodachi* until he can turn 180 degrees and be in *toi-maai*.

It is important not to stop the cutting action with the *kote* strike; a feint would cause a broken sequence. As you make your first attack, capitalize on the *motodachi*'s reaction to make your next attack.

FIGURE 6.3. *Nidan-waza combining kote-uchi and shomen-uchi.*

FIGURE 6.4. *Do-uchi.*

DO-UCHI

Do-uchi, or the strike to the *do*, begins with kendoists in *chudan-no-kamae* and *issoku-itto-no-maai*, as in figure 6.4*a*; again, the *motodachi* is on the left. The action starts as the attacker takes a small step forward moving his right foot first, followed by the left (*okuri-ashi* method), keeping *chudan-no-kamae*. The *motodachi* reacts by stepping forward with his right foot and brings his sword to jo-dan-no-kamae. The attacker sees the opening on the *motodachi's do* and brings his sword upward to a point where he can see under his left hand while stepping forward one half step with his right foot. As the attacker brings his rear foot up in *okuri-ashi* method, he starts his downward cut on the *mo-todachi's do* (fig. 6.4*b*). The attacker must follow the same line down with his sword as if he were go-ing to cut the *motodachi's men*. The center-line cut to the *motodachi's men* is very short and is accomplished by moving the hands forward about one foot, an important hand movement that keeps the *motodachi's* hands up and his elbows away from his *do*.

The attacker now takes another small step forward using *okuri-ashi* and turns his hands slightly to his left so the edge of the blade is in line to cut through the *motodachi*'s *do*. As the attacker turns his hands, he simultaneously changes the angle of his attack to the *motodachi*'s *do* about 20–30 degrees to his left and cuts the *motodachi*'s *do* with the first six inches of his *shinai*. As the end of his sword cuts the *do*, the attacker steps off to his right with his right foot at about a thirty-degree angle, followed by his left foot (fig. 6.4c). The attacker follows through with his cut. As he passes by the *motodachi*, he should be shoulder to shoulder with him and maintain eye contact as long as possible. When the attacker loses eye contact, he turns his head forward and continues on a straight forward path using *tsugi-ashi* footwork (fig. 6.4d; *tsugi-ashi* is described in chapter 8). The attacker continues to advance after the cut until he is in at least the *toi-maai* before he turns, faces the *motodachi*, and takes *zanshin*.

In executing *do-uchi*, do not bend at the waist; maintain your navel in an upward position. Keep the tip of your sword up; do not allow it to point at the floor during or after the *do* cut. Be sure to *kake-go*: "Do!"

Other than the tsuki, the *do* cut is perhaps the most difficult to execute properly. In *kenjitsu*, where the *do* or body cut was done by sinking the hips, it was considered the most dangerous cut to perform in a duel as it almost always exposed the attacker's head. Chiba Sensei once said, "The *do* was used most of the time as a secondary target because of the danger involved in executing it properly unless you were dueling or practicing with an inexperienced swordsman."

DEBANA-WAZA

The term *debana-waza* refers to any strike that takes advantage of the opponent's movement of attack. A *debana-waza* is performed quickly at the very instant your attacker moves toward you to execute his own attack. In the split second after the attacker moves, he is usually concentrating so completely on his own *waza* that he loses sight of your cutting action. This creates a void in his attack and allows the *debana-waza* to be performed. The particular *debana-waza* described here, *men-debana-men*, is the best *waza* to start with because it forces you to stretch forward while keeping your back straight.

This *waza* starts in *issoku-itto-no-maai* and *chudan-no-kamae*, as in figure 6.5a; the *motodachi* is on the left. The *waza* starts with the *motodachi* moving forward on his right foot and bringing the tip of his *shinai* up and away from your center and throat (fig. 6.5b). You need not move your feet at this point but must maintain *chudan-no-kamae*. By figure 6.5c the *motodachi* has fully committed to his attack on your *men*. You react quickly by moving forward on your right foot using *okuri-ashi* footwork and strike his *men* (fig. 6.5d); your sword cuts his *men* a split second before he completes his cut.

FIGURE 6.5. *Debana-waza: men-debana-men.*

Men-debana-men is difficult to practice initially because both kendoists have become attackers and both feel they have succeeded in the first cut. As you become more proficient, however, and as your eye and timing improve, the *waza* will become clear. To prevent the swords from colliding, if the attacker is cutting your *shomen* on the center line, simply cut his right or left *yokomen* on your *debana* movement.

OJI-WAZA

Oji-waza is a broad range of techniques that includes *suriage-waza* and *harai-waza*. *Oji* means to respond and *suriage* means to parry, or deflect your opponent's sword, by using the side of your sword in a rising, sliding movement. An *oji-waza* is thus a technique in which you stop the opponent's attack by parrying and then counterattack. On a real sword or *bokuto* the *shinogi* is used in this parrying motion.

The *oji-waza* demonstrated in figure 6.6 is an example of *suriage-kote*, or parrying to the glove. The *motodachi* is on the left; both kendoists begin in *issoku-itto-no-maai* and *chudan-no-kamae* (fig. 6.6a).

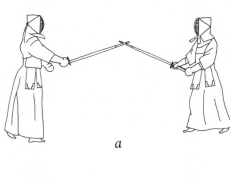

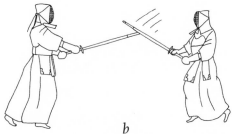

The *motodachi* steps forward with his right foot, keeping *chudan-no-kamae* and using *ayumi-ashi* footwork. The attacker responds with suriage on the *motodachi's* sword by rotating his hands counterclockwise while simultaneously moving his *kensen* (or, if using the *shinai*, his *sakigawa*) up no higher than the *motodachi's* eyes and stepping forward with his right foot, using *okuri-ashi* footwork (fig. 6.6b). The *motodachi* completes his attack to his opponent's *men*. The attacker corrects the angle of the cutting edge on his *shinai* by rotating his hands clockwise to their original position and cuts the *motodachi's* right *kote* (fig. 6.6c). After completing his *kote* cut, the attacker continues moving forward until he has passed the *motodachi* on his right side to a point where he can turn 180 degrees, face the *motodachi* in the *toi-maai*, and take *zanshin*.

FIGURE 6.6. *Oji-waza: the parry to the kote.*

When applying the *suriage-waza*, use both hands and simultaneously snap your wrists. Also, the cut to the *kote* occurs simultaneously with your right foot hitting the floor on your forward movement. This allows your whole body to make the cutting action rather than just your arms. Again, keep your back straight; do not bend at the waist. You do not always have to wait for your opponent to attack; as he moves forward or back you can step and parry his sword with *suriage-waza* on the right or left side of his *shinai*. This parrying motion gives you a chance to attack *men*, *kote*, *tsuki*, or *do*. Always try to parry your opponent's sword near its middle so as to force it off center.

Harai-waza is similar to, though simpler than, *suriage-waza*; it involves tapping your opponent's *shinai* without the rotating motion of *suriage-waza*.

NUKI-WAZA

Nuki-waza is a technique of evading the opponent's attack, then counterattacking. There are seven variations, of which the first is described in detail here:

1. *Kote nuki men*
2. *Men nuki men*
3. *Men nuki do*
4. *Kote nuki* right or left *men*
5. *Men nuki kote*
6. *Kote nuki kote*
7. All *katate-waza* (one-handed techniques)

Figure 6.7*a* shows the defender on the left side trying to avoid the attacker's *kote* cut by pulling toward himself with his right hand and not moving his feet. This is incorrect.

In figure 6.7*b* the defender has stepped back with his rear (left) foot (or at an angle to his rear) using *ayumi-ashi*, *okuri-ashi* right or left, or *hiraki-ashi* right or left. With his foot *waza*

FIGURE 6.7. *Nuki-waza.*

he simultaneously pushes up and out with his left hand, thereby causing the attacker's cut to fall on empty air. The defender's hands should continue up until his left hand is just above his eyes. At this point he steps forward with his right foot followed by his left and cuts the attacker's *men*. After completing the *men* cut, he continues moving forward using *ayumi-ashi* footwork and passes the attacker on his right side. He continues forward until he can turn 180 degrees, come to *toi-maai*, and take *zanshin*.

Figure 6.7c shows another incorrect *nuki-waza*. The body is bent and the kendoist is cutting with too much *shinai*. It is important to pay strict attention to your *ashi-waza* (foot technique) when applying *nuki-waza*. The back or side movement must be combined with the hand movements. When you step forward to apply your cut, combine these movements again with no break in the action. I find that moving to the left and using *hiraki-ashi* footwork works best for me. Do not allow your heels to touch the floor, so that your stepping back is only preparatory to your move forward. Stay relaxed and do not allow the opponent to discover your predetermined *waza*.

TAIATARI

In *kenjitsu*, using the real *katana* (long sword), *taiatari* (body collision) would be the most dangerous place to be in a conflict. Even if you killed your attacker, the chances of not getting cut to pieces in *taiatari* are slim—that is, unless you crash in quickly and come out immediately, applying your own *waza* such as *taiatari-hikimen, taiatari-hikikote,* or *taiatari-hikido.*

A detailed discussion of *taiatari* could justify a book by it-self. Here I would simply like to cover some of the basic "dos" and "don'ts."

Taiatari usually occurs when two kendoists have attacked unsuccessfully, not followed through with their attack, and come together as in figure 6.8*a,* which illustrates the correct way to execute *taiatari.* Each kendoist is trying to control the opponent's center with his *shinai* and left hand, using his right hand as a pivot point. Figure 6.8*b* shows an improper way to come out of *taiatari,* by placing the *shinai* on your opponent's shoulder and sliding it down while stepping back. This act could draw a penalty from the referees under the 1995 All Japan Kendo Federation Refereeing Guidelines. Figure 6.8*c* illustrates another prohibited act if it is used unfairly to shove your oppo-nent outside of the match court. Figures 6.8*d* and *e* show the

a

b

c

FIGURE 6.8 (*a–c*). *Taiatari.*

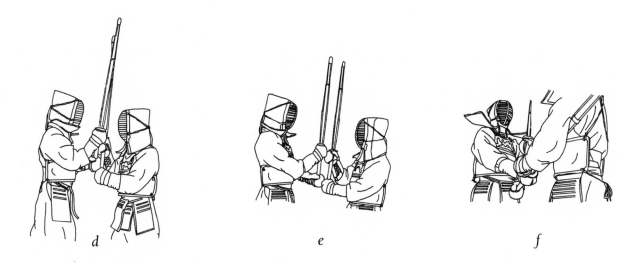

proper moving of the hands up and down to escape from *taiatari*. In figure 6.8*f* the kendoist on the right has placed his left arm over his partner's *shinai* in an attempt to hold it while he applies his own technique. This is a prohibited act if it is done intentionally. Figure 6.8*g* does not reflect a prohibited act, but it does reflect improper hand and body position: the hands are too low and the kendoists are too far apart to move properly.

In figures 6.8*h* and *i* the kendoist on the left is using his hands properly to move his partner's *shinai* out of the center line while using *hiraki-ashi* to move from side to side, trying to upset his partner's posture and balance. In figure 6.8*j* he has broken his partner's posture and, using *ayumi-ashi*,

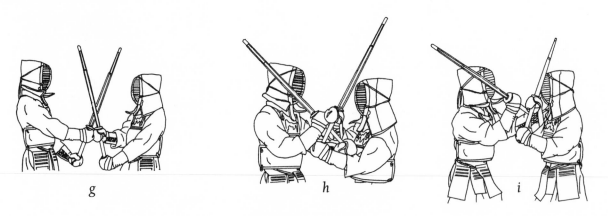

FIGURE 6.8 (*d–i*). *Taiatari.*

j

steps back with his left (rear) foot followed by his
right while simultaneously pushing upward on his
partner's right front hand. This movement allows him
to retreat one more small step. Trying to recover, the
kendoist on the right steps to his rear also (fig. 6.8*k*).
Seeing an opening in his opponent's *men*, the kendoist
on the left steps forward to execute a proper *men* cut
(fig. 6.8*l*). He follows through on the left side of his
partner until he can turn 180 degrees, come to *toi-
maai*, and take *zanshin*.

It is also permissible to step straight or to the rear
foot (either right or left) and execute a strike to your
partner's *men*, *kote*, or *do*. This is called *hiki-waza*.

k

l

FIGURE 6.8 (*j–l*) . *Taiatari*.

These basic movements are the elements from which the kendoist must draw. Mastering these cuts or strikes will improve the skills needed to react and change his attacks and defenses quickly in accordance with his attacker's cuts and thrusts.

7

A BRIEF HISTORY OF KENDO KATA

IT seems fitting to introduce this chapter on *kendo kata* by quoting a passage that was originally prepared by the Southern United States Kendo and Iaido Federation (quoted by permission):

> Modern Kendo bears but a faint resemblance to its feudal origin of sword wielding samurai warriors which are today depicted in movies and television. Kendo, literally translated, "the way of the sword," cannot be traced to a single founder or given an exact founding date. The story of the rise of modern Kendo begins with the samurai and extends over the culture of several centuries.
>
> By the end of the 12th century, the authority of the Japanese central government had declined. Bands of warriors grouped together for protection forming local aristocracies. Feudalism had come of age, and was to dominate Japan for

several centuries. With the establishment of the Shogun in Kamakura and military rule controlling Japan, a new military class and their lifestyle called bushido, "the way of the warrior," gained prominence. Bushido stressed the virtues of bravery, loyalty, honor, self discipline and stoical acceptance of death. Certainly, the influence of Bushido extended to the modern Japanese society and Kendo was also to be greatly influenced by this thinking.

Unlike the European knight and the Dark Ages of Europe, the Japanese warrior had no contempt for learning or the arts. Although Kenjutsu, "the art of swordsmanship," had been recorded since the 8th century, it gained new prominence and took on religious and cultural aspects as well. Sword making became a revered art. Zen and other sects of Buddhism developed and the samurai often devoted time to fine calligraphy or poetry.

The next great advance in the martial arts occurred during the late Muromachi period (1336–1568), often called the "Age of the Warring Provinces" because of the many internal conflicts. This period brought an increased demand and respect for men trained in the martial arts. Consequently, many schools of Kenjutsu arose, eventually numbering about 200. Each was taught by a famous swordsman whose techniques earned him honor in battle. Real blades or hardwood swords without protective equipment were used in training resulting in many injuries. These schools continued to flourish through the Tokugawa period (1600–1868), with the Itto-Ryu or "one sword school" having the greatest influence on modern Kendo.

Kendo began to take its modern appearance during the late 18th century with the introduction of protective equipment: the men, kote, and do, and the use of the bamboo sword, the shinai. The use of the shinai and protective armor made possible the full delivery of blows without injury. This forced the establishment of new regulations and practice formats which set the foundation of modern Kendo

With the Meiji Restoration (1868) and Japan's entry into

the modern world, Kendo suffered a great decline. The samurai class was abolished and the wearing of swords in public outlawed. This decline was only temporary, however. Interest in Kendo was revived first in 1877 when uprisings against the government showed the need for training of police officers. Later the Sino-Japanese War (1894–1895) and the Russo-Japanese War (1904–1905) again encouraged an awareness of the martial spirit.

Consequently in 1895, the Butokukai, an organization devoted to the martial arts, was established. In 1911, Kendo was officially introduced into the curriculum of the schools and in 1912, a set of regulations for Kendo, the Nihon Kendo Kata, was published. In 1939 as Japan prepared for war, Kendo became a required course for all boys.

After the war, because of its nationalistic and militaristic associations, Kendo was outlawed and the Butokukai was disbanded. However by 1952, supporters of Kendo successfully introduced into the public school curriculum a "pure sport" form of Kendo called Shinai Kyogi which excluded militaristic attitudes and some of the rougher aspects of practice characteristics of pre-war Kendo. Today Kendo continues to grow under the auspices of the All Japan Kendo Federation, the International Kendo Federation, and federations all over the world.

Although the outward appearance and some of the ideas have changed with the changing needs of the people, Kendo continues to build character, self discipline and respect. Despite a sportslike atmosphere, Kendo remains steeped in tradition which must never be forgotten. For here lies the strength of kendo which has carried it throughout history and will carry it far into the future.

Kendo is not a sport. One should never say, "We play kendo," as many do. One who "plays" kendo has lost the true meaning, along with the real spirit, of the art. One trains in kendo, or one might practice kendo, but one should never merely play at kendo. Jirokichi Yamada, who died in 1931, explains in the *Kendo ron* (Treatise on Kendo, or Moral Essence of Kendo) that a sport takes only a small portion of one's life, whereas kendo takes it all. Awake or sleeping, kendo is always working in your mind and body. When you practice a sport, you imagine yourself being victorious over or bringing amusement to another person. But in kendo, you must first be victorious over yourself; you must defeat your opponent without using your sword. As many Japanese kendo masters would say, you must have an immovable mind or heart, called *fudoshin*, and immovable wisdom, called *fudochi*. *Fudochi* does not necessarily mean being immobile like a mountain, but means having a mind that is not slow in leaving its surroundings; that is, it is always alert to constant changes. For example, suppose five armed men attack you. If you comply with each attacker's movement, not allowing your mind to stay with what you do, forgetting one move to deal with the next, you should be victorious in dealing with each attacker one at a time.

Yagyu Munenori, from the Yagyu Ryu Shin-hisho school of swordsmanship, wrote in the *Heiho kaden sho kinsei geido ron* (the Yagyu family's *Book of Swordsmanship*), published in 1716: "In order to become a master of swordsmanship, mere technical knowledge is not enough. A man must delve deeply into the inner spirit of it. He must obtain the state of mind known as *mushin* [no mind]." Training in any martial art becomes successful only when the student has absorbed the techniques into his subconscious. Then using them becomes purely instinctive. No thought processes are required. His attitude is one of receptivity: alert, but calm and fearless, with no preconceived idea of the outcome. One must create a consciousness free from thoughts, reflections, or distractions of any kind. This is often likened to a lunar reflection in water. Neither the moon nor the water is conscious of producing the effect known as "the moon in water." The water reflects accurately all images within its range; so a calm mind, like undisturbed water, can perceive all physical and psychological reactions of an opponent and respond appropriately. You are said to have mastered the art when the technique works through your body as if independent of your conscious mind.

All this has direct applications to learning *kendo kata*. If you practice *kata* as you "play" kendo, you will never understand it. I had a friend, a longtime practitioner of judo, who because of injuries had to quit judo and decided to pick up the sword. He called me from his home up north and asked about kendo teachers in his area and how to start. Before we hung up I told him to let me know if he needed anything and that I would be happy to help in any way I could. About eight months later he called and complained that his kendo *sensei* would not teach him all the *kata*. I said, "What do you mean?"

He replied, "The *sensei* will only show me the first seven *kata*. Every time I ask him about the other three, he says 'later.' What's the matter with him, Mr. Craig?"

"I don't think there is anything wrong with him. He just wants you to perfect the first seven—that's all."

"But I know those first seven *kata* like the back of my hand, and I'm tired of doing them over and over."

"There are no tricks in *budo*, only perfection," I said. At this he hung up. "Too bad," I thought, "he could have been a good kendo man."

No matter what you decide to do in life, you must master the fundamentals. The key to anything you undertake lies with basics. Moreover, an instructor cannot make you learn anything but can only show you the way. You must teach yourself. You must discipline yourself and never stray far from the basics in each practice. Most people find the martial arts hard to learn, not just because they're inherently difficult, but because people only want to "take a course" in them. They come to my dojo and say, "I'd like to try kendo." What does that mean? I'd like to try getting married? Or, I'd like to try this job? My belief is: if you have not committed yourself to learn, how do you expect me to show you the way? Unfortunately, this is how most people travel through life. They try this, and then that, not really learning anything.

Kendo has been the father to most other Japanese martial arts. It has left the richest and most enduring legacy and, in so doing, has made the greatest contribution to the Japanese spiritual culture. It is the most elegant and culturally rich of all the arts, but, in my opinion, it is also the hardest to learn. Some people who have not mastered the basics might win a match or two, or maybe even a tournament. But this kind of luck can not continue; without mastering the basics, which can be done only with the technical and spiritual guidance of a good teacher, it disappears with time. The skill of the teacher is always reflected in the student, even when the student becomes his own person. If the teacher has built a sturdy foundation, it will always be there for everyone to see. Though a book can be a helpful tool, it can never replace a professional teacher.

Kendo had its greatest growth during the latter part of the Muromachi period (1393–1572). Not only did kendo become organized, but the *sensei*–disciple relationship became deeply embedded in the new kendo schools. Kendo instructors and instruction fell into two categories: battle *kenjitsu*, where the sole purpose was to kill, and the new dojo kendo, called *ryuha* (loosely translated as an extension of the *ryu* or style), where the purpose was the refinement of technique and the expansion of theories. Dojo kendo became more popular with the rural samurai and the wealthy samurai than it did with the battle-tested warrior, and it was through the *ryuha* that most of Japan's famous swordsmen emerged. Tsukahara Bokuden of the Bokuden Ryu, who was one of the most outstanding samurai, came from a *ryu* and eventually opened his own *ryuha*. Even Miyamoto Musashi, founder of the Nito Ryu, started his kendo from a *ryu*. During his time, the time of the new Tokugawa government, known as the Edo period (1603–1867), the *ryu* began to fade and the *ryuha*, or new style, began to emerge.

Shusaku Chiba, founder of the Hokushin Itto Ryu, also lived

during the Edo period. Shusaku Chiba took lessons from his father in his old Chiba Ryuha before establishing and registering the new Hokushin Itto Ryu with the Bakufu or Tokugawa shogunate. During this time the influence of Zen, Confucianism, and Buddhism on the samurai became strong, and as a result, a driving force in Shusaku Chiba's practice of swordsmanship became the perfection of mind and body rather than the learning of combat technique.

Early in the eighteenth century the prototypes of the modern protective equipment (*kote, men, tare,* and *do*) were introduced along with the *shinai*. With these new inventions came teaching licenses and kendo ranks. Today these licenses and ranks are confirmed by the All Japan Kendo Federation and have no connection with the licensing or ranking policies of the different classical martial arts *ryu* such as the Hokushin Itto Ryu. The All Japan Kendo Federation licenses and ranks are based on criteria established by the Federation. The ranking system in modern *budo* adopted by Japan on March 27, 1971, establishes six novice classes of *kyu*, none of which has an age restriction. The *kyu* in ascending order are as follows:

6th class:	*Rokkyu*
5th class:	*Gokyu*
4th class:	*Yonkyu*
3rd class:	*Sonkyu*
2nd class:	*Nikyu*
1st class:	*Ikkyu*

Each rank above the *kyu* called a *dan*. The ten ranks, collectively called *yudansha,* are listed in table 7.1.

Traditionally, no person is sufficiently qualified to teach his particular art until he has reached the rank of *godan* or obtained a teaching license. The licenses, listed in table 7.2, are normally awarded on the basis of examinations by the applicant's national federation. To be awarded a teaching license, a person

TABLE 7.1

Rank	Age	Title	Time in Grade
1. *Shodan*	16 years and over	No formal title	At least 3 years as *kyu*
2. *Nidan*	17 years and over	No formal title	Over 1 year after *shodan*
3. *Sandan*	19 years and over	No formal title	Over 2 years after *nidan*
4. *Yodan*	25 years and over	No formal title	Over 3 years after *sandan*
5. *Godan*	35 years and over	Renshi	Over 3 years after *yodan*
6. *Rokudan*	40 years and over	Renshi	Over 5 years after *godan*
7. *Shichidan*	45 years and over	Kyoshi	Over 7 years after *rokudan*
8. *Hachidan*	55 years and over	Kyoshi	Over 8 years after *shichidan*
9. *Kudan*	60 years and over	Hanshi	Over 10 years after *hachidan*
10. *Judan*	70 years and over	Hanshi	Over 15 years after *kudan*

must have an outstanding character and must also be cited by his peers for exceptional achievement.

A student appearing before a board for the ranks of *shodan* to *sandan* must perform seven *kata* and may be required to perform as either *uchidachi* or *shidachi* using the *bokuto*. He is also required to perform free practice with a student junior to his rank and a student of the rank he is applying for. *Yodan* and above must perform ten *kata*, seven with the *bokuto* and three with the *kodachi*, and pass a written examination. The written exams usually consist of questions like: "State the purpose of learning kendo. What is kendo? Write a short paragraph on *kiryoku* (willpower) and another on *kokoro* (mind of kendo)." The exams usually end with questions about the regulations and refereeing of a kendo match. For the rank of *godan* and above the testing can often become quite

TABLE 7.2

Teaching rank	Title
1. Instructor	Renshi
2. Teacher	Kyoshi
3. Master teacher	Hanshi

complex and the written exam very lengthy on refereeing and regulations.

Unfortunately, as kendo becomes more popular, it is being exploited. Some exponents are skilled and others are not; therefore, if you are contemplating starting classes in kendo or *iaido*, and especially *kenjitsu* or *iaijitsu*, you should ask to see the instructor's credentials. Very few teachers outside Japan have the authority to teach some old *ryu* of *kenjitsu* or *iaijitsu*. You can check the legitimacy of someone's claims to a teaching license from a legitimate *ryu* with Japanese roots by writing to:

Kobudo Shinko Kai
5-3 Kojimachi
Chiyoda-Ku
Tokyo 102 Japan

With respect to kendo or *iaido*, you can write to the kendo federation in your region, or if you cannot find its address, to the Executive Secretary of the All United States Kendo Federation:

Mr. Tim Yuge
c/o AUSKF
P.O. Box 2004
Lomita, CA 90717
Phone: (800) 957-5363
Fax: (310) 543-2489
E-Mail: yuge@mizar.usc.edu

Or write to:

All Japan Kendo Federation
Hongo-2-35-21
Bunkyo-Ku
Tokyo 113 Japan

Few non-Japanese exponents of kendo are qualified to teach. Often, self-declared experts in swordsmanship reveal their confusion between kendo and *kenjitsu, iaido* and *iaijitsu.* Watch out for statements like, "Oh, kendo, that's just a sport. What I teach is the real thing, *kenjitsu.*" Then they will smother you with Japanese terminology to cover their lack of experience. These self-proclaimed swordsmen do not have Japanese credentials to support their claims and, most likely, have never been to Japan, let alone studied under a professional kendo teacher. If you come across someone who has a lot of beautiful oriental credentials on his wall, ask to take a picture of them and then have someone translate them. A friend of mine and I

Sensei and I demonstrating iaijitsu in 1981.

once did this with someone who claimed rank from China in kung fu. The certificates turned out to be a Chinese laundry list. When we went back to confront the instructor, he had closed his school and disappeared.

A legitimate instructor won't mind questions if they are asked respectfully and should be happy to supply you with whatever you need to make up your mind. Invest a little time before you invest your money.

❖

O Sensei once told me a story about *kendo kata* involving a samurai named Soyu Terada (1745–1825). An elderly kendo *sensei* of the classical manner—that is, he didn't believe in wearing the new kendo protectors—Terada Sensei trained in the old-fashioned way, through *kata* with *bokuto* or sword. One day, Terada Sensei was challenged by a group of modern kendoists who wore the protective gear. When he accepted their challenge, they laughed and said he was foolish, that he slept in the past with his old-style *kata* movements, and that they would soon awake him with a few sharp blows from their *shinai*. When the day came for the match, Terada Sensei showed up with only his *bokuto* and squared off with the champion of the opposing side.

"Where is your *bogu*?" the champion proclaimed.

"I have never engaged in a kendo match with *bogu*," Terada Sensei replied. "I have only engaged in real matches with real swords. I do not use such things, but your side can use all the protective armor you need. Please come strike me with all your strength and knowledge."

Terada Sensei stood lightly but firmly with his *bokuto* in the *chudan-no-kamae* posture. The champion looked at Terada Sensei and thought, "I'll hit his *shomen*: he has no protector and that will be the end of this foolishness." But just as the champion had this thought, Terada Sensei spoke out in a loud clear voice, "If you attempt to strike my head, I will cut your *do*." The champion stepped backward startled. So it went each time the champion had a thought of attack. Terada Sensei would voice it out loud and then explain his counter. Finally, at his wit's end, the champion sat down, overwhelmed. One by one Terada Sensei disposed of the rest of the group the same way. Terada Sensei accomplished complete victory without ever using his *bokuto*.

Shusaku Chiba, who witnessed this episode by request of Soyu Terada, later wrote, "Only after I saw the great Terada Sensei in action did I realize the true value of *kata* training without contact. The *kata* advocates have earned my deepest respect. At such a ripe old age Terada Sensei was one with the sword; only *kata* can do that."

The passage of time has brought, and will continue to bring, changes in *waza* and *kata*, no matter how hard one tries to maintain their original forms. Some aspects of *kata* have changed simply because of the disappearance of the samurai society that served so long as their basis. Before the All Japan Kendo Federation *kata* was established, there were no uniform methods suitable for conveying an understanding of timed decisive action, spiritual intent, and the beauty of the *waza*. All these aspects have been emphasized in the modern version of the federation's *kata*.

The original *kata* were based on the idea of fighting with a real sword to the death—win or lose, life or death. These deadly earnest events were called *shinken-shobu*. In *shinken-shobu*, victory or defeat depended on *sen*, combat initiative that depends on a state of mind in which the sword can be delivered quickly, accurately, and forcefully so as to take life with a single stroke. Once a *shinken-shobu* match was in progress, the samurai knew that only three outcomes were possible: *ai-uchi*, *katsu*, or *make*: respectively, mutual killing, victory, or defeat. This type of fighting is called old tradition, or *koryu*, practiced by the *kenshi*, or swordsmen of the old school. In the old *kata*, the stances were much wider and thus the hips much lower than in the new *kata*. Since the hips have been raised, the posture has changed, and the use and angles of the body in thrusting and cutting have changed as well. Chiba Sensei once told me that, in the early period of the Hokushin Itto Ryu, no cuts to the trunk were employed. In those days, cuts were made by dropping the hips. This caused the trunk to become farther away from the opponent's blade, making the trunk extremely dangerous to attack. If attacked, it exposed the attacker to *suki*, that is, creating and exploiting a weakness in the enemy.

It wasn't until Shusaku Chiba's time that a contestant, successfully striking his opponent's *do*, was considered to have defeated his opponent. Of course, as we have seen, by then *shinai* and *bogu* were being employed. The hips were much higher, and the *do* became more accessible as a target. Thus, from that time forward, the *do* became one of the main targets in *shinai* kendo. In modern kendo the body movement is a particularly difficult problem. Sensei often said it was most important to keep the old ways while walking on the new path, looking for perfection in the future.

Each *ryugi*, or style, had its strong and skillful swordsmen, called *kengo*, who tested that style's *kengi*, or sword *waza*, against those of other *ryugi*. Before the Togukawa rule in 1603, the kengo had the moral support of the government to use *shinken-shobu* to develop their sword technique at every opportunity. This was referred to as combat *kenjitsu* style and, in some circles, as the positive style of swordsmanship. With *shinken-shobu*, there was never any doubt which technique or style prevailed. To the samurai, it was the only way possible to test his swordsmanship. After 1603, when the peaceful centuries of the Tokugawa shogunate began, this combat or battlefield style of *shinken-shobu* fencing became illegal without government sanction, which was rarely given. Consequently, a new style of swordsmanship became popular. This new style had a "wait and see" attitude, taking advantage of *suki*, a weakness in the enemy. In this style, referred to as the valiant *ryu*, *kata* took over as the main training method of the *kenjitsu* dojos, although the prearranged formal exercises of the battlefield style of swordsmanship were maintained.

Yagyu Munenori, mentioned earlier, was a high-spirited swordsman of the seventeenth and eighteenth centuries with a true love for the battlefield style of fencing. In his view, the new "wait and see" style was becoming too popular, and the samurai who trained in it were becoming soft and confusing reality and fantasy. Having obtained permission from the shogun to test his skills against this style, he went to the Yoshiwara area of Edo and deliberately provoked a group of seven samurai by spitting on them. In the fight that followed, Yagyu killed two outright and severed the arms of two others. Three ran for their lives. Though Yagyu proved his point and became famous as a swordsman, he could not stop the popularity of the "wait and see" style of fencing. Consequently, the classical *ryu* that once featured the battlefield style of *kenjitsu* were forced to adopt it.

After the mid-seventeenth century, the majority of the dojos proceeded along this path but also maintained the old *ryu's kata*. Generally speaking, though, according to Chiba Sensei, the sword experts of any particular *ryu* knew only a few *kata*. In fact, some great swordsmen might know only four or five. As Gichin Funakoshi, an old master, said in *Karate-do ichiko*, an expert swordsman used to "keep a narrow but plow a deep furrow. Present-day students have a broad field but only plow a shallow furrow."

By the middle of the eighteenth century there were three types of sword practice, called *keiko*: with the *shinai*, the *bokuto*, or the *katana*. When swordsmen of different *ryu* wanted to test their respective skills they did so in contests called *taryu-jiai*. In these contests they used a *katana* or *bokuto*, and the matches almost always ended up with crippling injuries or needless death. It wasn't long before the government banned this type of contest, which forced the samurai to rely on the *shinai* to test their skills. This type of combat, which is still in existence today and is called *shinai-shiai*, reinforced the *kata* training in old *kenjitsu* dojos. According to the records of the Jikishin Ryu, formed in the eighteenth century, *kata* was the first step in learning swordsmanship in that *ryu*. Numerous young men of that time were drawn into dojos that featured *kata* and *shinai-shiai*. Participation in mock combat allowed the young men to imagine they were fighting with real swords like so many of their ancestors. By the nineteenth century *shinai-shiai* was so popular that more than five hundred schools of swordsmanship were specializing in it. Unfortunately, by the end of the Edo period, most kendo dojos were owned and operated by commoners, who felt that this new *shinai* fashion of swordsmanship allowed them to share in the glory of the samurai traditions that had been reserved for the classical warriors. These new types of dojos emphasized and trained solely for the purpose of winning exhibitions or matches in a sportlike atmosphere. If it had not been for the old traditional dojos like the Hokushin Itto Ryu, Japan might have lost forever the classical *kata* that are so cherished today.

In about 1830, not too long before the fall of the Togukawa era, a samurai of the battlefield style of fencing named Otani Seichiro introduced Shusaku Chiba to an official of the Mito government dojo in Edo. Shortly thereafter, the Mito-Han officials adopted the Hokushin Itto Ryu, which is a battlefield style of fencing, as their official style. This appointment gave great prestige to the Chiba clan and, once again, to the battlefield style of fencing. One of Chiba's students, named Ryoma, a samurai of the *goshi* or country class (see the appendix), had such skill with the *shinai* that he would freely tour throughout Japan in *dojo-yaburi* fashion (literally, "dojo storming"), challenging anyone to *shinai-shiai*. It was through these escapades that thousands of students flocked to Edo to enroll in the Hokushin Itto Ryu, which Shusaku Chiba Sensei operated at the Gembukan Dojo. When I was in Japan in the 1970s I practiced at the Imperial Dojo. While there, my instructor pointed out Shusaku Chiba's name plaque, along with hundreds of other outstanding instructors, all in rows along the wall. I could almost see them practicing *kata* there through the mist of long ago. Thinking back about all this, I am reminded of what one of my students once said: "To practice *kata* is so hard, I hope we don't grow too fond of it."

Before delving into the *kata* in the next chapter, I want to address several matters that are required in order to get that "certain feeling" when performing *kata*. These are things that make your *kata* different from someone else's. When you perform *kata*, keep in mind the mental and behavioral aspects of each side while performing the proper movements. When you, as *shidachi*, are standing in *chudan-no-kamae* at the beginning of each *kata*, think of the following before moving to meet the *uchidachi's* sword: *ichigan*, *nisoku*, *santan*, and *shiriki*, or simply "eyes, feet, courage, and strength of the opponent." Looking at your opponent correctly is called *metsuke*. There are two parts to *metsuke*: moving the eyes and fixing the gaze of the eyes. Chiba Sensei always said, "Look at his eyes first to determine his intentions, strength, and courage. Then look at the *kensen* of his sword and hands; they will move against you after his mind has determined what action he will take. An inexperienced swordsman's eyes will look at the target first. But when you're fencing an experienced swordsman, you must look behind his eyes into his mind and force him to reveal his attack, so that you can determine beforehand his movements." Be careful with your own *metsuke*, because when your eyes move and what they observe are both of great importance. If you are the *shidachi*, you must think of yourself as the enemy, the *uchidachi*. If you are the *uchidachi*, you must become your enemy mentally, the *shidachi*. Miyamoto Musashi once said, "In strategy, fixing the eyes means gazing at the man's heart."

A lot of old kendo *sensei* talk about the four weaknesses in

In the late nineteenth century the Hokushin Itto Ryu became noted for its use of the iron fan (tessen) in kendo techniques. A samurai named Yoshitsone, a folk hero in many old Japanese stories, defeated Musashi-Bo-Benkei by using his tessen to parry Benkei's spear attacks. Benkei, a noted samurai in his own right, was so impressed by Yoshitsone's tessen movements that he became his devoted follower. Probably the most noted samurai using the iron fan were from the Yagyu Ryu, who were instructors to the Tokugawa shogun.

martial arts: doubt, fear, confusion, and surprise. They are created by the conscious mind, and the practice of martial arts is a continuous battle with ourselves to overcome them. The All Japan Kendo Federation has a saying: "Kendo is to discipline the human character through the application of the *katana*." In other words, kendo and other martial arts should teach us how to deal with and control these four weaknesses.

1. *Doubt*. You have doubt when your opponent's actions are difficult to understand or when you think too much about how strong your opponent is acting. You overcome doubt by the practice of *uchikomi* and *kiai*. The word *kiai* simply means that the spirit of one martial artist has joined in battle with the spirit of another at the height of the attack or defense. The Japanese word itself suggests a togetherness (*ai*) with spirit (*ki*). If you block out the conscious mind with your *kiai*, only the subconscious remains to perform. Here is where your practice and repetition of attack and defense pay off.

2. *Fear*. Fear is caused by the ego-fear of losing; fear of not looking good when performing the *kata* in front of your peers. Fear causes the muscles to stiffen and the shoulders to tighten and become rounded. Sometimes even the legs tremble. One never really eliminates fear, but with the correct spiritual strength that forms the basis of technical skill, one can conquer it. Then attack and defense become merely a matter of reflex. Swordsmanship demands instantaneous reaction to action. There isn't time to stop and look at death or think of victory. One should train with as many people as possible, so you can learn to foresee their action and react accordingly. Chiba Sensei taught, "It is only natural to have some fear at first, but when you reach *toi-maai* clear your mind and do not allow the attacker to feel anything but your sword and training."

3. *Confusion.* Confusion and doubt walk hand in hand. The two together are extremely dangerous; they will be a swordsman's downfall. Confusion by itself makes the swordsman unable to perform the simplest movements. More important, it leaves him unable to make quick judgments. Confusion is mainly caused by not having enough confidence in one's own ability. Never allow your mind to hesitate between the defense and offense; half of the block is the attack. If you breathe half a breath between the two, you have hesitated and created confusion.

4. *Surprise.* Surprise is simply caused by someone doing something unexpected or unforeseen. Surprise can be reduced and almost eliminated with *metsuke.* Surprise works on the mind quickly, making it impossible for you to find an opening and apply the proper technique. *Metsuke,* on the other hand, means not only looking at the opponent and into his intentions but also absorbing everything around you while not concentrating on any one thing. Miyamoto Musashi once said, "If you look to the left, you will forget the right. If you look at the opponent's hand, your mind will think of only his hand; if you look at his foot, your mind will think of only his foot." If your eyes are distracted or focused on one thing, your mind moves to that object and becomes imprisoned by it. On the other hand, if your eyes see everything without focusing on any one thing, while penetrating into the attacker's intentions, his slightest movements and attacks can be foreseen with the greatest accuracy. Always remember: sound comes first no matter how slight; sight comes second; touch is third. In other words, first you hear it, then you see it, then you feel it. Sensei always taught, "When you hear the sword cut through the air, but just before you see it, lies your cut or attack and defense. If you feel it, you haven't practiced enough."

❖

8

TECHNICAL KATA

THE seven *kata* described in this chapter constitute the long sword portion of the All Japan Kendo Federation *kata*. A mastery of these seven forms will take the kendo practitioner to the level of *sandan* and should establish the groundwork for an understanding of how *kendo kata* is performed. Yet the descriptions offered here cannot supplant study with a qualified teacher. Rather, this material may serve as an aid in the learning process and, I hope, inspire some readers to seek out a true kendo *sensei*.

The seven long sword *kata* described herein are *ipponme*, *nihonme*, *sanbonme*, *yonhonme*, *gohonme*, *ropponme*, and *nanahonme*. Before proceeding to the descriptions, however, it remains to discuss a few more basic aspects of kendo technique.

DATOTSU

Although *datotsu* (cutting and thrusting) is done with the first six inches of the blade, you must pay strict attention to the direction of the *tsuka*. Gripping the *katana* (long sword) is similar to holding the *bokuto* or *shinai,* with one significant difference: when gripping the *katana,* you mustn't allow your index finger to touch the collar, called the *fuchigana.* There must be a separation the width of two or three fingers between the front and rear hand. The right hand is closest to the *tsuba,* while the left hand grasps the *kashira.* Hold the sword securely with the last two fingers of both hands and relax the remaining fingers. The knuckles of the index fingers and thumbs must point upward. There should be a small amount of tension in the little fingers and the next two fingers; the index fingers and thumbs remain loose. While performing *kata* or *waza* the hands should never be removed from the *tsuka.*

Keep the elbows loose and slightly away from your sides. The shoulders and elbows should be relaxed so they can move freely. The arms and elbows, especially on the left side, should be extended outward about three-fourths of their full extension. Always stand and move with your lower back and hips pushed slightly forward while keeping your back straight; it is most important that you not lean. Squeezing your buttocks together while moving will help keep your back straight. Your abdomen should be slightly tightened, your chest out, and your head erect. It is important that your posture be natural, so do not strain. Your mind should be relaxed, while your body is prepared to move in any direction at any moment. When you move, you should do so calmly and without disturbing your stability. This basic, natural standing posture is called *shizentai* and is the basis for all other positions in kendo, whether it be the *sonkyu* position or the *kamae* basic posture.

After thrusting or cutting, always keep a keen eye on the opponent. Never look away or allow your mind to wander. You must stay alert for an unexpected movement. This alertness is called *zanshin.* After you have executed the proper *datotsu,* the most important part of kendo is the *zanshin.* It separates the real from the unreal, the practitioners from the expert. As Sensei always said, "If you're asking me whether I am faster or quicker than you, I don't know. But if you're asking me whether I can kill you, the answer is yes."

Your cut should be like a flash of lightning. Charge the opponent with your whole mind and body and focus all your strength and power in that one flash of light. After completing the cut, you should relax and assume the proper *kamae*. Your *kiai* should come spontaneously with the cutting action and from the lower part of your stomach, not just your throat. In kendo there is a saying, "*kiken taino itchi.*" This simply describes the cutting action or *datotsu* that unites *ki* (spirit, vigor, active physical and mental strength) with *ken* (*waza* or technique for attacking) and *tai* (posture, overall attitude). In other words, your thrusts and cuts should be done simultaneously with correct, clean techniques, with a strong *kiai* that calls out your attack, and with correct footwork. To practice *kendo kata* properly, you must do all of the above and follow up the attack with *zanshin*.

The kendoist who can achieve total unity of mind, sword, and body has truly achieved mastery—*uwate*. When practicing kendo or *kendo kata* you must strive to have these three elements in combination. Using one or two without the other will result in poor swordsmanship and poor *kata*. Only through repeated practices, with the *suburi* (wooden long sword) as well as the *uchikomi-ningyo*, *uchikomi-bo* and *uchikomi-dai*, will you achieve the skill of *ki-ken-tai-itchi*, "spirit-sword-body in one strike." Of course, practicing with a top instructor is the final stage of any *uchikomi* training, and nothing can take the place of old knowledge. The goal you must set for yourself in kendo and *kendo kata* is not to win matches or impress your peers but to develop perfect cuts and thrusts through the development of these three elements: mind, sword, and body. Always remember: anyone can cut with his arms and hands, sometimes with a certain amount of skill to an untrained eye. The experienced swordsman will cut from his waist. While the distinction may appear slight, it represents the difference between the person who has devoted his time and the person who has devoted his life.

ASHI-WAZA (FOOTWORK)

Most kendo instructors will agree that, to understand your opponent, you must establish a working relationship with his mind and sword. This can be accomplished by imagining a single strand of hair connecting his *kensen* with yours. You must follow his movements through these connected tips. If he advances, you must retreat straight back or at a slight angle to either side. If he retreats, you must follow without hesitation so that the hair connecting you is never broken. The way you connect yourself and your *kensen* to your opponent will determine the failure or success of your *waza*. You must develop the ability to know or at least to feel what your opponent is going to do before he does it.

The position of your feet while in *chudan-no-kamae* or while performing *kata* is important. With toes pointing forward, your right foot should be ahead of your left and the toes of your left foot aligned with the heel of your right. Your feet should be approximately eight to ten inches apart (fig. 8.1*a*). Your body weight should be slightly forward at a point just between the center of your feet. The heel of your right foot should be raised just enough to slide a piece of paper under it. The left foot should be lifted naturally about one-half inch so that your weight is distributed forward. When I was first learning kendo my instructor taped a thumbtack—point up—under my left heel so I would maintain the correct heel height. I don't recommend this. Figure 8.1*b* and *c* illustrate improper alignment of the feet and excessive raising of the heels.

To move forward promptly, push with the left foot, similar to the way the rear wheels push a vehicle (fig. 8.2). Remember to keep the toes of both feet pointing forward and the knees slightly bent. Do not allow your left foot to slide in front of your

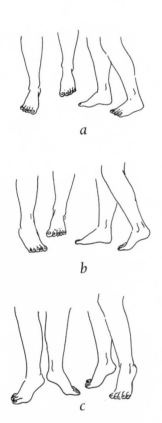

FIGURE 8.1. *Correct (a) and incorrect (b and c) positions of feet in chudan-no-kamae.*

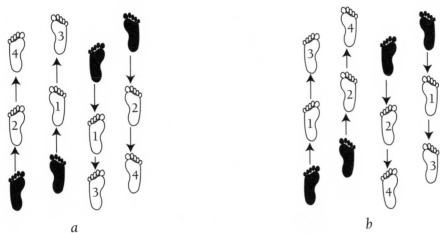

FIGURE 8.2. *Okuri-ashi and ayumi-ashi (forward and backward).*

right foot, unless it is so designated in the *kata*. This stance should be practiced continually until you are able to move quickly and effortlessly forward and backward without losing your *shizentai*.

The foot patterns shown in figures 8.2 and 8.3 should be practiced constantly; they are the very foundation of kendo, whether *kata* or free practice with *bogu*. *Okuri-ashi* (fig. 8.2*a*) is used in short-range movements forward or backward. *Ayumi-ashi* (fig. 8.2*b*) is used for covering great distances quickly forward or backward. A variation of *okuri-ashi*, used in short-range movements right or left, is used in making cuts and thrusts (fig. 8.3*a*). *Hiraki-ashi* (fig. 8.3*b*), a swinging foot movement to the right or left, is used in the defense of thrusts and cuts. *Tsugi-ashi* (fig. 8.3*c*) is a forward foot movement used to deliver cuts and thrusts at a greater distance.

The footwork most used in kendo today is *okuri-ashi* and *hiraki-ashi*. *Okuri-ashi* can be used in connection with many *waza*, since it covers distances of one or two steps to the front, rear, right, left, and diagonal front and back. It is the main position in *kendo kata* for advancing and retreating and

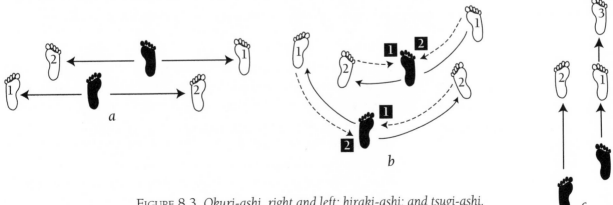

FIGURE 8.3. *Okuri-ashi, right and left; hiraki-ashi; and tsugi-ashi.*

for starting and finishing each *kata.* To learn this *ashi-waza,* advance the foot corresponding to the direction you intend to move, whether forward or backward, then immediately bring the opposite foot to the one you have just moved.

Hiraki-ashi means "open footwork." If you wish to move to the left, move the left foot first, followed by the right. To move right, the right foot moves first, followed by the left. Twist your left or right hip, depending on which way you move, so you are turned toward and facing your opponent directly. This footwork is used extensively throughout the *kendo kata.*

In performing your *ashi-waza* never allow your heels to touch the floor and never lift your feet too far off the floor. Your feet should slide across the floor as in roller or ice skating. The balls of the feet come in contact with the floor first. Your hips stay under your balance point at all times, allowing you to move in a straight horizontal line. *Ashi-waza* is designed to help the student, whether novice or advanced, develop maximum efficiency while delivering thrusts and cuts. I cannot overemphasize the importance of practicing it diligently.

UCHI-WAZA

The most important thing to remember about *uchi-waza,* or striking technique, is that all cutting is done with the legs, hips, and left hand; the right hand is just a guide to the target. With your feet placed as in figure 8.1*a,* extend your arms straight out in front of you and interlock your fingers as in figure 8.4. While stepping forward and backward using *okuri-ashi* (fig. 8.2*a*), keep your arms relaxed and swing them over your head in rhythm with your foot movements. After several repetitions, squeeze your fingers and hands together quickly. If you are right-handed your left wrist will bend to the left; if you are left-handed just the opposite will occur. Either way is incorrect. Neither wrist should bend. When the exercise is executed correctly, your wrists will be straight and in the center of your body.

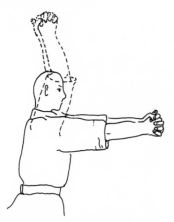

FIGURE 8.4. *Basic uchi-waza.*

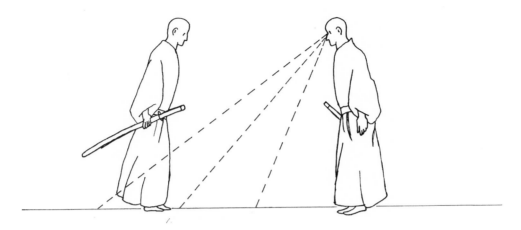

FIGURE 8.5. *Metsuke.*

Metsuke refers to the position of the eyes before or while executing a sword *waza.* You should be focusing on nothing but seeing everything—especially your opponent's eyes. The eyes are the windows to the mind. With proper *metsuke* you will also be able to keep the proper *maai* with your attacker. Proper eye contact and *maai* should bring your mental focus and spiritual intent to its peak, while helping you develop your *ki-guri* (pride). More than a physical act, *kendo kata* involves *ki,* the pursuit of spiritual beauty. This pursuit, which the Japanese refer to as the heart or spirit of the art, starts with *metsuke* and ends with *zanshin. Ki* nurtures a sense of strength and dignity; one who has it will perform the *kata* with calmness, agility, and grace. *Zanshin,* on the other hand, is an unbroken concentration after the attack is finished. *Zanshin* reflects the advanced stage of power and dignity a kendoist reaches after many years of practice.

FIGURE 8.6.
Chudan-no-kamae, front view.

FIGURE 8.7.
Chudan-no-kamae, side view.

BASIC POSTURES

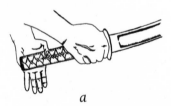

a

Figure 8.6 and 8.7 depict *chudan-no-kamae*. *Chudan* means "center," *no* is a word like "of," and *kamae* means an attitude of the body, a "ready posture" or "position." When we speak of the body being in a *kamae*, we are speaking of not only a physical position but more importantly a spiritual one; the spiritual and physical aspects of kendo are inseparable. *Chudan-no-kamae*, or center position, probably the most effective posture in kendo, allows the greatest variation for attack and defense and thus is considered the basis of the other five postures. Though it may look simple, it is perhaps the hardest to master.

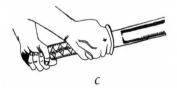

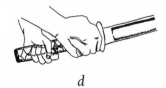

b   *c*   *d*

FIGURE 8.8. *Correct and incorrect sword grips.*

When moving in any direction in the *chudan-no-kamae* position, maintain your left hand in the center of your body near your navel (fig. 8.6) and the tip of your sword pointed at your opponent's throat. It is important that you should have a feeling of forward movement. Your knees should be slightly bent.

To perform *chudan-no-kamae* move your right foot forward (fig. 8.2*a*), with your left hand positioned about one fist width from your abdomen near your navel, and your right hand about one and one-half fingers from the sword guard. Figures 8.8*a–c* illustrate the correct grip; figure 8.8*d* is incorrect. The little finger of the left hand holds the *tsuka* firmly while the left index finger holds only slightly. The right hand holds the *tsuka* about one fist forward of the left hand. The middle knuckles of the index fingers and the thumbs point upward. The thumbs remain loose. All cutting action is done with the left hand; the right hand is only a guide. Hold the elbows loosely but do not allow them to touch your sides or project outward. They must have adequate latitude to execute any cut or thrust you may require. The *katana* is held so that the *kissaki* (tip) points outward and toward the *uchidachi's* throat. Keep your shoulders relaxed and both heels off the floor.

There are several varieties of *jodan-no-kamae*, or upper position, each with its own name and usage determined by the position of the feet and hands. For example, if both hands are on the *tsuka*,

    a   *b*

FIGURE 8.9. *Hidari-jodan-no-kamae, front and side views.*

    a   *b*

FIGURE 8.10. *Migi-jodan-no-kamae, front and side views.*

FIGURE 8.11. *Gedan-no-kamae, front and side views.*

FIGURE 8.12. *Hasso-no-kamae, two side views.*

the term *morote* is used; if only one hand, the term *katate* is used. Either the left hand and foot or the right hand and foot may be forward; one might also have the right foot and left hand forward. Of all the different types, the standard is the *hidari-jodan-no-kamae*, or left upper position, a two-handed posture with the left foot forward that is effective for both defense and offense (fig. 8.9). You can move from *chudan-no-kamae* to *hidari-jodan-no-kamae* and vice versa with ease. From *chudan-no-kamae*, advance your left foot while simultaneously lifting your right hand to a point just above your forehead and approximately in the center of your head. Your left hand is just high enough that you can see your opponent under it. Some teachers say that if you tied a string to your left wrist with a lead weight at the end, it would fall directly over your left foot. Be sure to push out and up with your left hand at the angle shown in figure 8.9*a*; do not pull back with your right hand when stepping forward with your left foot.

In *migi-jodan-no-kamae*, or right upper position, the sword is more directly over your head (fig. 8.10). Remember to maintain the proper *metsuke*, as described above.

Figure 8.11 depicts *gedan-no-kamae*, or lower position. From *chudan-no-kamae*, lower your *kensen* until it is pointing forty-five degrees toward the floor, or approximately at your opponent's knees. Do not move your feet. The right foot remains forward. Maintain the proper *metsuke* and be sure to stay alert for any movement the *uchidachi* might make. This posture is used in all the *kata* when retreating to your starting position after the *waza* is completed. It is also used as a defense and offense in the *kata sanbonme* and *ropponme*, discussed later in this chapter.

Like *jodan-no-kamae*, *hasso-no-kamae* (fig. 8.12) has many variations; the one described here is used in the *kata*. Starting in *chudan-no-kamae*, advance your left foot forward while bringing both hands to the upper right side of your face. The *tsuba* is about level with your mouth, as in figure 8.12*b*, and your left fist is approximately even with your right breast. The blade is tilted slightly to the rear. *Metsuke* is the same as described above. *Hasso-no-kamae* is used in *kata yonhonme*, described later in this chapter, and is frequently used in *keiko* (practice) in modern kendo.

Waki-no-kamae (fig. 8.13) also has several variations, but again I will discuss only the one we will use in the *kata*. Starting in *chudan-no-kamae*, move your right foot to the rear while bringing both hands to your right side. Your left hand is in line with your navel; your right hand is just a little below the right hip. The *metsuke* is the same as for *chudan-no-kamae*. Waki-no-kamae is used in *kata yonhonme* and *kodachi nihonme*.

a

b

FIGURE 8.13. *Waki-no-kamae*.

MAAI

Martial artists strive to maintain a correct distance, or *maai*, between themselves and the attacker or practicing partner. In kendo, the three basic distances are called near interval, or *chikai-maai*; one-step interval, or *issoku-itto-no-maai*; and distant interval, or *toi-maai*. The corollary distances in karate would be the distance at which your opponent could strike you by taking one step backward; the distance at which he could strike you by taking one step forward; and the distance at which he could strike you by taking more than one step forward, respectively.

Chikai-maai is the distance so small that you are unable to cut or thrust correctly without taking one step to the rear. In some cases you use *chikai-maai* when waiting for your opponent to step backward so you can move quickly forward and deliver a cut or thrust. *Chikai-maai* is also used when applying *hikimen*, which consists simply of waiting for your opponent to step forward, then using either *hiraki-ashi* or *okuri-ashi* (that is, stepping straight back or diagonally to the rear) and delivering a cut to the attacker's *men*. More complex techniques such as *hikikote* can sometimes be applied to deal with *chikai-maai*, as in the second *kendo kata, nihonme.* The use of *kake-go*—not just a *kiai* but more of a high-pitched yell or shout—is important here. It pushes your spirit and unbalances your attacker.

Issoku-itto-no-maai, the interval at which the first inch or two of your swords have crossed, allows you either to cut your attacker by taking one step forward or to avoid his attack by taking one step backward. Almost all kendo matches begin and end with this interval, which is used throughout the *kendo kata* to avoid the *uchidachi*'s attacks. Some teachers call this distance *uchi-ma*, or cutting interval. It is the *maai* in which you must be most alert; Chiba Sensei called it the most dangerous interval, the one in which the dual will be won or lost.

Toi-maai, the distant interval, is usually called *to-ma* in kendo and is used to control your attacker's *kensen* and the center of the attack. In this *maai* you are relatively safe from attack because the attacker has to move at least two steps forward to launch his attack. Chiba Sensei told me that in the old days this was the most commonly used *maai*. Today, only the more experienced swordsmen use this *maai* in training. When at *toi-maai* or *chikai-maai* the more skilled kendoist (the *uwate*) has advantage over the less skilled kendoist (the *shitate*) because the *shitate* feels he is at a safe interval.

BOWING

With the completion of the basic postures, it's time to turn once again to the bow. As we discussed in chapter 3, there are two bows in kendo, the standing bow (*shizentai rei*) and the kneeling bow (*seiza rei*). Both are done as a prelude to *kata* and *keiko*.

Some people mistakenly think that the bow is an act of worship. Rather, the *rei* is a symbol of respect for the traditions and teachers who have gone before you. It indicates that both practitioners are willing to put aside their differences and cooperate with each other during the *keiko*. This holds especially true for *gakaku-geiko*, practice between kendoists of equal ability.

Shizentai rei is the standing bow without sword. Stand normally with your feet at a forty-five-degree angle, heels almost together, your knees unlocked. Your hips are in line with your abdomen and are slightly tensed. Your shoulders and arms are relaxed and your back is straight. Your chin is slightly tucked but your neck is in an upright position. Do not strain. Your eyes are straight forward, your arms and hands at your sides. Now bend at the waist and allow your hands and arms to move forward to the front of your legs. Your hands slide down your legs until the fingers touch the tops of your knees. Stop. Your head is now in line with your shoulders and your eyes are looking at the floor about five feet to the front. Do not bend your neck to accomplish this. As you bend, do so calmly and slowly so you do not disturb your stability. Usually, I count to five at this point and return to an upright position. This natural *rei* is the basis for all the others: kneeling, standing,

FIGURE 8.14. *Seiza rei*

sonkyu, or *kamae*, with or without the sword. When you have the sword in your left hand, thumb on the *tsuba* cutting edge up, the right hand travels downward and the sword hand travels slightly upward. Your eyes are now on the *uchidachi*; however, do not bend your neck to accomplish this.

Seiza rei is the formal kneeling bow with *hakama sabaki*. Because kendo is practiced while wearing a *hakama*, it is important that you have complete control of the skirt portion so it will not hinder your movement. As you start downward with your left leg into *seiza*, take the palm of your right hand and brush aside the left trouser leg of your *hakama* from the inside to the outside so that it rests behind your left knee. As you continue downward, simultaneously use the back of your right hand against your right inside pant leg. These movements should be done unobtrusively and smoothly.

To assume *seiza*, hold the sword in your right hand, thumb on the *tsuba*, cutting edge up. You are standing erect, breathing normally and quietly through your nose. Bend both knees outward so you can widen the space between them. Bending slightly forward, apply *hakama sabaki* with your left hand as your left knee comes to rest on the floor, followed by your right. Your toes are now under you, and you are almost sitting on your heels. Straighten your insteps and cause your right big toe to come to rest on top of your left big toe. Turn your heels outward while maintaining your insteps on the floor. Lower your hips until your buttocks come to rest on the inside bottom of your soles. Be sure your weight is distributed evenly over your calves. Your shoulders should be relaxed, your chin slightly tucked while you remain sitting erect. Bring the sword to your right thigh just forward of your right hip bone. Now place your sheathed sword on the floor with the cutting edge to you, *tsuba* even with your right knee (fig. 8.14).

Things to remember when starting to sit in *seiza* with a sword or swords:

1. Do not bend too far forward when applying *hakama sabaki*.
2. Keep your thumb on the *tsuba* to prevent the sword from sliding out of the *saya*, or sheath.
3. Place the left knee on the floor first, then the right, in a smooth flowing motion.
4. Do not drop quickly or bang your knee on the floor.
5. Maintain approximately two fists' distance between your knees while in *seiza*.
6. Do not allow your *saya* to hit the floor.
7. Hold the sword parallel as you sit so the *kojiri* (the tip of the *saya*) does not strike the floor.
8. *Metsuke* is on your partner, seeing nothing in particular, yet seeing everything.

Perform the bow with complete dignity. Do not hurry it, but do try to execute it in a smooth, flowing action. While keeping your buttocks in contact with the back of your calves and your back straight, slowly start bending forward at the waist. As you start this forward motion slide your left hand forward, palm down, on the floor in front of you, followed by your right hand in a similar fashion, forming a triangle with the hands (fig. 8.15a). Continue bending forward, keeping your back straight (fig. 8.15b). The *uchidachi* keeps an eye on the *shidachi's* movement, bowing just a little lower than the *shidachi*; it would be impolite for the *uchidachi* to stop his bow before the *shidachi* does. When the *shidachi* stops, the *uchidachi* pauses a moment; then, as the *shidachi* starts to return to an upright position, the *uchidachi* does the same (fig. 8.15c). Your hands slide up your thighs in a reverse order: right hand first, followed by the left hand (fig. 8.15d).

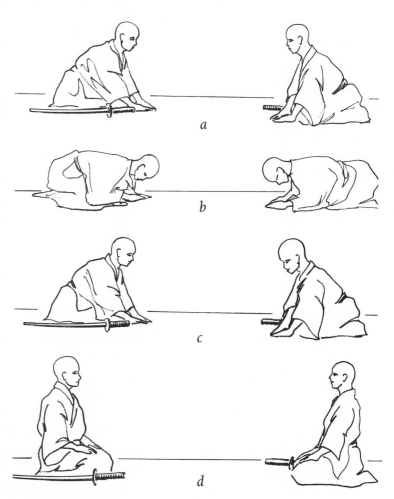

FIGURE 8.15. *Movements of the shidachi and uchidachi during seiza rei.*

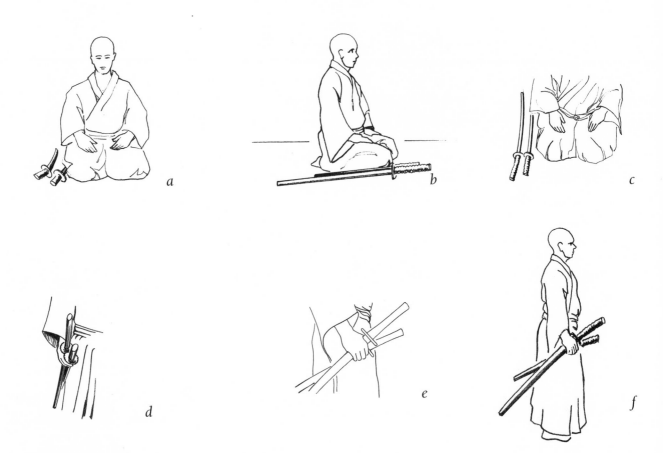

FIGURE 8.16. *Handling the daisho.*

Figure 8.16 shows how to handle the *daisho,* or long and short swords, when portraying the *shi-dachi.* Figures 8.16*a* and *b* are front and side views of the *shidachi* in figure 8.15*d.* The *kodachi* is next to you with the *katana* to the outside, both cutting edges are toward you, and the *tsuba* are even with your right knee. Figure 8.16*c* shows that, as you start to rise from *seiza,* you reach with your right hand to the *kodachi* while reaching with your left hand across your body. Place the *kodachi* in your left hand, keeping it on your right side. Now pick up the *katana* with the last three fingers of your right hand, starting with the little finger, and bring it to your right hip. Place the *kodachi,* cutting edge up, between your right thumb and index finger. The *tsuba* of the *kodachi* should rest behind the *tsuba* of the *katana.* Starting with your right leg, rise and align the ball of your right foot with your left knee. The toes of your left foot are under the ball of your left foot. The swords should be resting on your right hip. Now push with your left foot and rise with the right leg, pushing upward. Do not lean forward; rise as gracefully as possible. Bring your left foot to your right. Your right arm should hang naturally at your side (figs. 8.16*d* and *e*). The *uchidachi* should take hold of the *katana* just below the *tsuba* with the right hand and rise to a standing position as I have explained for the *shidachi* and simultaneously with the *shidachi*. Be sure that the *tsuba* are secured with your thumb before rising and that all swords maintain a small slant backward. This way, the blades will not slip out of the sheaths (fig. 8.16*f*).

At this time both the *shidachi* and the *uchidachi* turn, together and smoothly, toward the *kamiza* and bow. The *shidachi* turns to the left at a 135-degree angle, the *uchidachi* to the right at a 45-degree angle. The *shidachi* starts with his right foot and takes as many steps as needed to reach point 1 in figure 8.17. He then turns 135 degrees to his right, kneels down with his right knee, reaches across with his left hand, takes the *katana*, and lays down the *kodachi* with the cutting edge inward toward his leg and the *tsuba* about even with the left (front) foot (fig. 8.18).

The *shidachi* now changes the *katana* back to his right hand, cutting edge up. The sword should be at about a 45-degree angle as he rises, bringing his right foot to his left (fig. 8.19). While the *shidachi* is completing these movements, the *uchidachi* moves at a 45-degree angle to point 2 in figure 8.17. He then turns 135 degrees to his left. The sword is still in his right hand in a natural position, slanting downward at a 45-degree angle with the cutting edge up. The *uchidachi* moves smoothly and waits for the *shidachi* to complete his extra movements and move to point 3 in figure 8.17. The *shidachi* moves to point 3 by simply moving his left foot forward and to the left approximately one step, followed by his right foot. Point 3 is about a 45-degree angle to the front and forward of point 1.

The *shidachi*, now facing the *uchidachi* (fig. 8.20), follows the *uchidachi*'s movements just a brief moment later from this point on throughout the entire *kata*. This is to differentiate student from teacher and aggressor from defender. They bow and

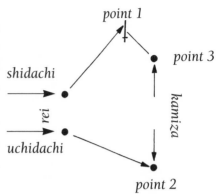

FIGURE 8.17. *Relative positions of the shidachi and uchidachi during seiza rei.*

FIGURE 8.18. *The shidachi kneels, takes the katana, and lays down the kodachi.*

FIGURE 8.19. *Position of katana in the shidachi's right hand (front and side views).*

FIGURE 8.20. *The shidachi faces the uchidachi.*

bring the *katana* in their right hands to the front and center and insert the *saya*, cutting edge up, into the left side of the *obi* (fig. 8.21). *Maai* at this point should be approximately nine normal steps apart, that is, from point 3 to point 2 in figure 8.17.

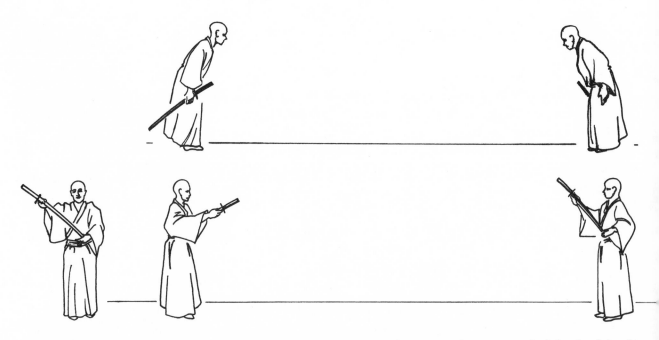

FIGURE 8.21. *The shidachi (front and side views) and uchidachi bow and insert the saya into the left side of the obi.*

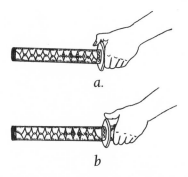

FIGURE 8.22. *Pushing the tsuba forward with the left thumb.*

The *shidachi* and the *uchidachi* now place their left thumbs on the *tsuba* (fig. 8.22). They then start forward with the right foot, taking three normal steps and pushing the *tsuba* forward with the thumb (fig. 8.23).

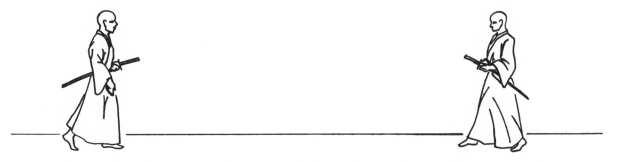

FIGURE 8.23. *The shidachi and uchidachi approach each other.*

As shown in figure 8.24, on the second step, they take hold of the *tsuka* with the right hand, turning the cutting edge of the *katana* with the left hand about twenty degrees counterclockwise.

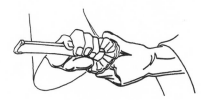

FIGURE 8.24. *Counterclockwise rotation of the katana.*

a   *b*   *c*

FIGURE 8.25. *Drawing the blade from the saya.*

On the third step (which is on the right foot), they start drawing the blades from the *saya*. As they reach their destination, they continue sliding the sword upward and outward until no more than three inches of the tip remains in the *saya*. This should be accomplished before bringing the left foot forward (fig. 8.25).

As they slide their left (rear) feet forward and their knees start to bend slightly outward and down, they use their right hands to bring the remaining tip of the sword forward and to the center of their bodies (fig. 8.26).

FIGURE 8.26. *Bringing the sword forward and center.*

FIGURE 8.27. *Moving to sonkyu position.*

As the *shidachi* follows the *uchidachi's* downward movement to *sonkyo* position, he takes hold of the end of the *tsuka* and starts in a downward movement until his left hand is in the center of his body near his navel. The tip of the sword will be pointing at the *uchidachi's* throat with the first two inches of the swords crossing (fig. 8.27).

Figure 8.28 shows *sonkyu* in side and front views. *Sonkyu* is an important starting position, and great care should be taken to learn it correctly. As the left (rear) foot comes forward, the knees bend outward. The toes point outward at a forty-five-degree angle, making a V shape. The heels should be off the floor so that they almost touch and are under the center of the body. The back should be straight, the eyes forward, chin tucked in slightly, and shoulders relaxed. The center of the buttocks should be over the center of the heels. O Sensei always said, "You can tell what kind of training a swordsman had by the way he sits in *seiza* or, most important, how he takes *sonkyu*."

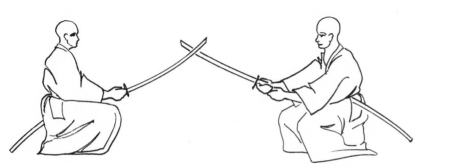

FIGURE 8.28. *Sonkyo position, side and front views.*

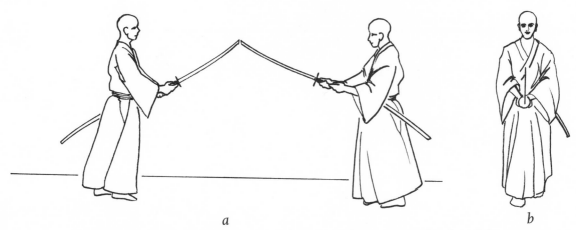

FIGURE 8.29. *Assuming chudan-no-kamae at the issoku-itto interval, side and front views.*

The *uchidachi*, then the *shidachi*, rises and assumes *chudan-no-kamae* at the *issoku-itto* interval (fig. 8.29). As you move upward to a natural standing position, do not allow your knees to lock, and step slightly back with your left foot (refer back to figs. 8.6 and 8.7). The *shidachi* should be looking at the *uchidachi*'s eyes while still seeing his entire body.

The *uchidachi* starts lowering his *kensen*. The *shidachi* follows until the tips of their swords are pointing downward at a forty-five-degree angle. They then turn the cutting edges of their swords slightly to the left so that the tips point at each other's left knee (fig. 8.30). The swords descend together with the cutting edge at a small angle to the left.

FIGURE 8.30. *Lowering the kensen, side and front views.*

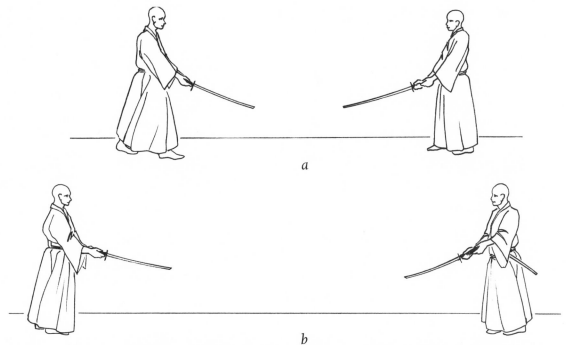

a

b

FIGURE 8.31. *Stepping backward to starting position, beginning and completion.*

With the *kensen* still pointing down, the *uchidachi* starts moving, followed immediately by the *shidachi*. As figure 8.31*a* depicts, they both move to the rear starting with the left (rear) foot, each taking five small steps backward. Figure 8.31*b* shows the completion of this movement. *Maai* should be nine normal steps apart, or approximately where you started (refer back to fig. 8.17).

The *uchidachi* assumes *chudan-no-kamae*, followed immediately by the *shidachi* (fig. 8.32). You are now ready to start the first *kata*, *ipponme*.

FIGURE 8.32. *Assuming chudan-no-kamae.*

FIGURE 8.33. *The shidachi and uchidachi at beginning of ipponme.*

IPPONME

FIGURE 8.34. *The shidachi at beginning of ipponme, left and front views.*

The *uchidachi,* on the right, moves first by moving his left foot forward and assuming a two-handed *jodan-no-kamae* (refer back to fig. 8.9 for *hidari-jodan-no-kamae*). The *uchidachi's* right foot does not move except for lifting the heel off the floor about one-quarter inch. The left heel is off the floor just enough that a piece of paper can slide under it. The *shidachi,* watching closely, sees the *uchidachi* move and follows immediately afterward by sliding his right foot slightly forward and assuming a right *jodan-no-kamae* (refer back to fig. 8.10 for *migi-jodan-no-kamae*). You are now in the position shown in figure 8.33.

Figure 8.34 shows the left and front sides of the *shidachi.* To accomplish *jodan-no-kamae,* be sure not to pull the *tsuka* with your right hand, but rather push out and up with your left (rear) hand in a circular motion. Your heels are off the floor, your shoulders are relaxed, and you are breathing normally.

The *uchidachi* begins on his left (front) foot and the *shidachi* on his right (front) foot. The *uchidachi* starts the action, and each person advances three steps. They meet at a *toi-maai* in-

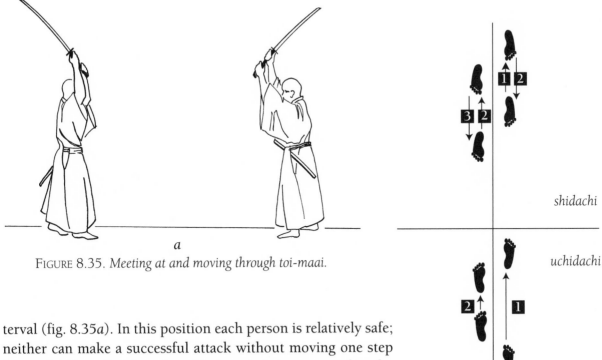

a

FIGURE 8.35. *Meeting at and moving through toi-maai.*

shidachi

uchidachi

b

terval (fig. 8.35*a*). In this position each person is relatively safe; neither can make a successful attack without moving one step forward. When first learning this *kata* it is important that the *uchidachi* stops completely and reconfirms this one-step attacking interval. However, there is no stop when performing the *kata*. As you advance in your understanding of this *maai*, the *uchidachi* simply continues through *toi-maai* by stepping forward with his right (rear) foot (fig. 8.35*b*). As the *uchidachi* arrives at *toi-maai* slightly ahead of the *shidachi*, he feels a weakness in the *shidachi's* defense. Taking advantage of this feeling, he does not stop but advances his right (rear) foot and delivers (in his mind) a cut to the *shidachi's* shomen.

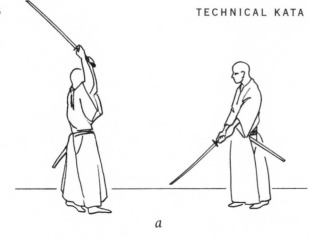

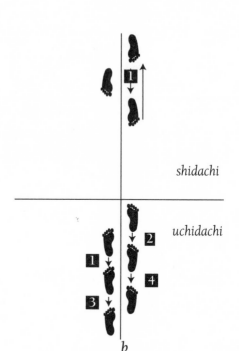

shidachi

uchidachi

FIGURE 8.36. *The shidachi avoids the uchidachi's cut.*

b

FIGURE 8.37. *The shidachi delivers a cut to the uchidachi's shomen.*

Figure 8.38. *The shidachi lowers his kensen to the uchidachi's eyes.*

The *shidachi* feels the threat of the attack and, as the *uchidachi's* sword moves downward and just before it strikes him, steps approximately one-half step to the rear with his left foot, followed immediately by his right. Keeping both heels off the floor, the *shidachi* pushes upward and to the rear with his hands, thereby avoiding the *uchidachi's* cut (fig. 8.36).

As the *shidachi* comes to a stop with his backward motion, he immediately slides forward, starting with his right (front) foot followed by the left, brings his hands down, and delivers a cut to the *uchidachi's* shomen (fig. 8.37). As the *uchidachi* makes his cut and misses, he pauses his *kensen* at the *shidachi's* neck. As soon as the *shidachi* starts his forward body movement, the *uchidachi* lowers the tip of his sword to *gedan-no-kamae*. The *uchidachi* accompanies his attack with the *kiai* "Yah!"; the *shidachi* accompanies his attack with the *kiai* "Toh!"

While the *uchidachi* is in *gedan-no-kamae* and after the *shidachi* has completed his cut, the *uchidachi* takes one-half step backward with his left (rear) foot, followed by his right. His heels are on the floor. The *shidachi* lowers his *kensen* to the middle of the *uchidachi's* eyes (fig. 8.38).

FIGURE 8.39. *The zanshin.*

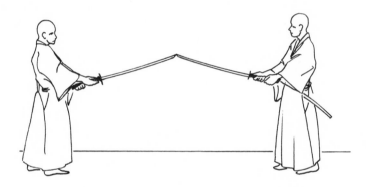

FIGURE 8.40. *Arriving at chudan-no-kamae.*

The *uchidachi* takes another one-half step to the rear starting with his left foot, followed immediately by his right, remaining in *gedan-no-kamae*. The *shidachi* advances his left (rear) foot forward and assumes *jodan-no-kamae*. The *shidachi* must be sure to push forward and upward with his left hand—not his right (fig. 8.39). This movement of the *kata* is the *zanshin*. It reflects the *shidachi's* mental attitude of being able to continue his attack.

With the *shidachi's* completion of *zanshin* and the *uchidachi's* feeling of being mentally released by the *shidachi*, the *uchidachi* starts an upward movement with his sword. The *shidachi*, seeing this action, immediately follows by stepping to the rear with his left (forward) foot and starts a downward movement with his sword. Both the *uchidachi* and the *shidachi* should arrive at *chudan-no-kamae* simultaneously (fig. 8.40). The *shidachi* must take an adequate step to the rear with his left foot to achieve the correct *maai*, with no more than two inches of the sword tips crossing. The *uchidachi* does not move his feet from their last positions.

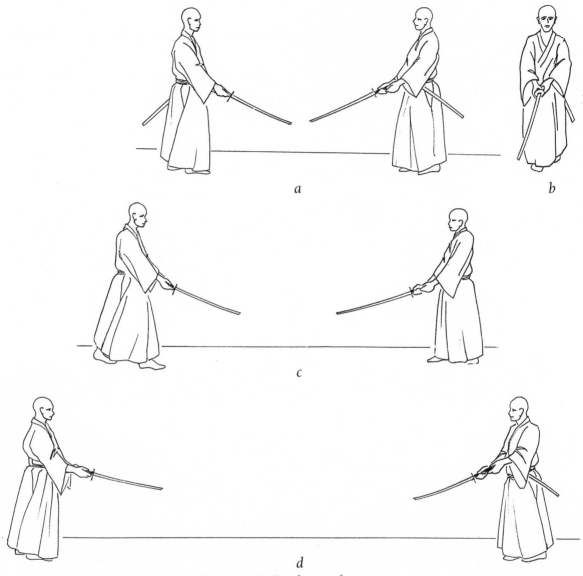

a   *b*

c

d

FIGURE 8.41. *Conclusion of ipponme.*

From *chudan-no-kamae*, the *uchidachi* initiates the movement, followed immediately by the *shi-dachi*. The *uchidachi* starts to lower his *kensen* to *gedan-no-kamae* (fig. 8.41*a*). Each person now turns the cutting edge slightly to his left, so that the *kensen* is pointing at the left (rear) knee of each opponent (fig. 8.41*b*). With the *uchidachi* initiating the movement, each person takes five small steps to the rear starting with his left foot (fig. 8.41*c*). As they arrive at the starting positions (approxi-

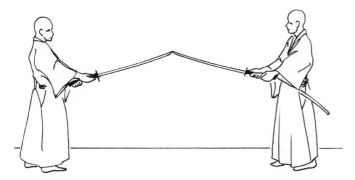

FIGURE 8.42. *Toi-maai at the beginning of nihonme.*

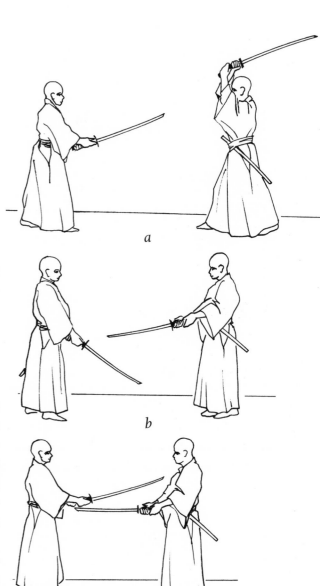

a

b

c

FIGURE 8.43. *The uchidachi cuts to the shidachi's right wrist.*

mately nine normal steps apart), the *uchidachi* assumes *chudan-no-kamae*, followed immediately by the *shidachi* (fig. 8.41*d*). This completes *ipponme kata*.

NIHONME

The *uchidachi* and the *shidachi* begin *nihonme kata* nine normal steps apart, as at the end of *ipponme*. Both have taken *chudan-no-kamae*, right feet forward. Remaining in this position, each person takes three steps forward, starting with his right foot, until he arrives at *toi-maai* (fig. 8.42; the *uchidachi* is on the right, the *shidachi* on the left). The right feet are forward and heels are slightly off the floor.

The *uchidachi*, looking for a weakness in the *shidachi's* defenses, pauses. When he detects an opening, the *uchidachi* slides his right foot forward followed immediately by his left while simultaneously bringing his sword to a high posture, almost *jodan* (fig. 8.43*a*). The *uchidachi's* left fist pushes straight outward and up-

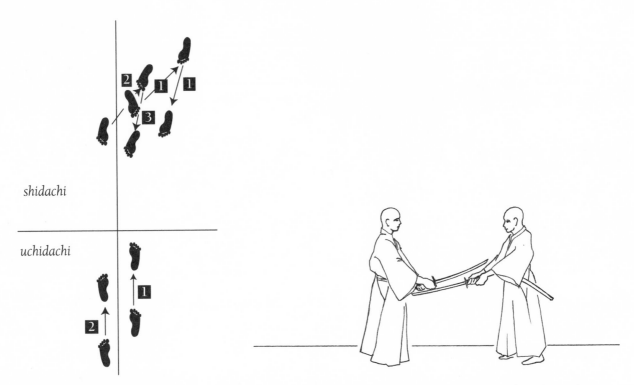

FIGURE 8.44. *Footwork for the cuts to the right wrist.*

FIGURE 8.45. *The shidachi cuts to the uchidachi's right wrist.*

shidachi

uchidachi

ward until it is just above his eyes—that is, where he can just see under his fist. He then delivers a cut to the *shidachi's* right wrist, kiaiing "*Yah!*" As the *uchidachi's* cut is in its downward path, but just before it makes contact, the *shidachi* lowers his *kensen* and steps with his left foot diagonally to his left, followed by his right foot (figs. 8.43*b* and 8.44). The *uchidachi* finishes his cut and stops his sword just below the *shidachi's* right wrist (or where his wrist would have been). The *uchidachi* should not allow his sword to travel much farther than this; his sword should be almost parallel to the floor (fig. 8.43*c*).

With his right foot, the *shidachi* steps forward diagonally. As he advances, he delivers a cut to the *uchidachi's* right wrist by swinging his sword upward and then downward, kiaiing "*Toh!*" as he delivers his cut. The *shidachi's* sword movement stops as his left foot comes to a completed forward movement (figs. 8.44 and 8.45). The *shidachi's* sword should stop about one-half to one inch above the·*uchidachi's* wrist. The *shidachi* should keep his heels off the floor.

Bill Smith Sensei, fifth dan and shidachi (right), and Rick TheBerge Sensei, fifth dan and uchidachi (left), performing nihonme.

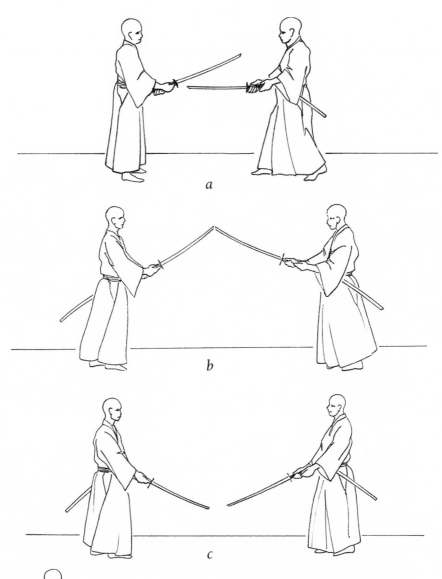

a

b

c

FIGURE 8.46.
Lowering the
swords
in nihonme.   *d*

Upon the completion of the *shidachi's* cut and after being mentally released by the *shidachi's zanshin*, the *uchidachi* steps with his left foot, followed by his right, to his rear approximately one-half step. As he does so, he keeps his sword under the *shidachi's* sword (fig. 8.46a). The *shidachi* follows the *uchidachi*, stepping to his right, starting with his right foot and fol-

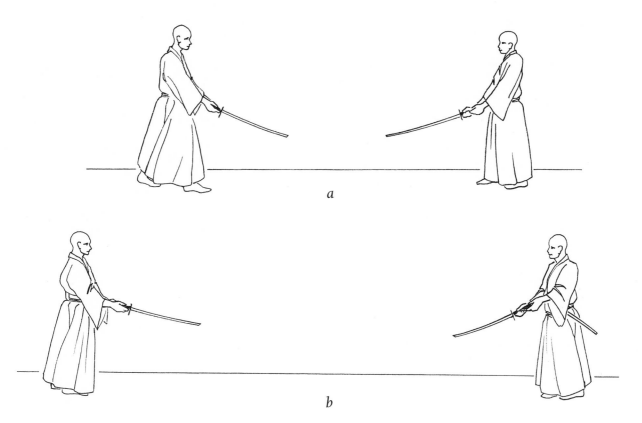

FIGURE 8.47. *Conclusion of nihonme.*

lowed by his left foot. Both assume *chudan-no-kamae* and are in *issoku-itto-no-maai* (fig. 8.46*b*). In figure 8.46*c* the *uchidachi* has started lowering his sword, followed by the *shidachi*, to a low posture. When the tips of their swords are about even with each other's left knee, they turn the cutting edges of their swords to the left (fig. 8.46*d*).

Starting on the left (rear) foot, the *shidachi*, following the *uchidachi*, takes five small steps to the rear to the correct *maai* (fig. 8.47). They assume *chudan-no-kamae* and are now ready for the next *kata*.

SANBONME

Figure 8.48*a* shows the *uchidachi* and the *shidachi* in *chudan-no-kamae* at the normal interval; the *uchidachi* is on the right and the *shidachi* is on the left. Each has his right foot forward. The *shidachi* watches his attacker intently for the slightest movement. The *uchidachi* starts his sword in a downward movement and the *shidachi* follows until they are both in *gedan-no-kamae* (fig. 8.48*b*). Begin-

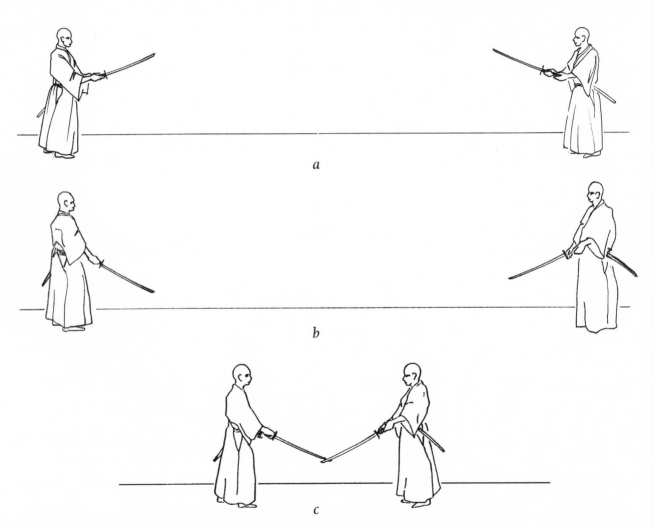

a

b

c

FIGURE 8.48. *Sanbonme: the initial approach.*

ning with the right foot, the *uchidachi* starts forward, followed by the *shidachi*, both staying in *gedan-no-kamae*. Each takes three steps forward, maintaining the *kiarasoi*, or spirit of combat. They arrive at *issoku-itto-no-maai*: the one-step cutting interval (fig. 8.48c).

The *uchidachi* starts his sword upward slowly, the *shidachi* following immediately, until they both arrive at a point slightly below *chudan-no-kamae* (fig. 8.49a). While moving their swords upward, the *uchidachi* senses a weakness in the *shidachi's* defense and chances an attack. The *uchidachi* directs the *kensen* of his sword to the left side of the *shidachi's* sword, slides forward with his right foot followed immediately with his left, tries to deliver a two-handed horizontal *tsuki* to the *shidachi's* solar plexus, and shouts "*Yah!*" (fig. 8.49b).

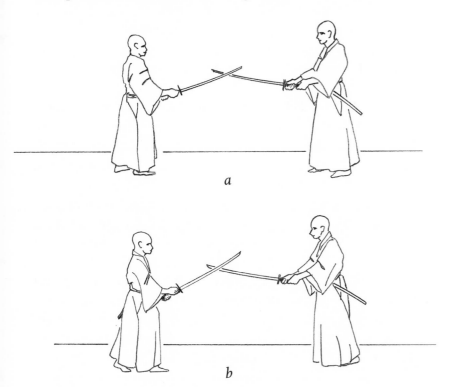

a

b

Figure 8.49. *The uchidachi attacks.*

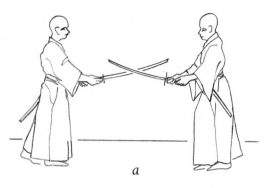

a

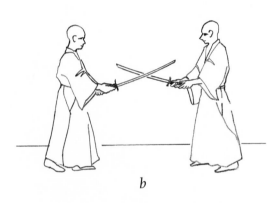

b

c

FIGURE 8.50. *The shidachi advances.*

As the *uchidachi* makes his attack by sliding his sword's *shinogi* (a raised edge running down either side of the blade) along the *shidachi's shinogi* and extending his arms forward, the *shidachi* takes one step to his rear with his left foot, followed immediately by his right. The *shidachi* applies a small amount of pressure with the *shinogi* of the *monouchi* (first four inches of blade) of his own sword against the *uchidachi's* sword. This is done by keeping the *kensen* at the center of the *uchidachi's* throat while turning your hands and blade slightly to the left (clockwise). Keep the *kashira* or end of the *tsuka* in the middle of your body and your forearms slightly away from your body. Also keep your shoulders relaxed and your back straight. This movement on the *shidachi's* part will turn the *uchidachi's* sword and parry the attacking thrust. This *kata* can become extremely dangerous if not practiced slowly and with the proper *maai*.

The *shidachi* now steps forward on his right foot followed by his left and, using his arms and hips slightly, thrusts his sword forward, yelling "*Toh!*" This movement puts the *shidachi* one-half step closer to the *uchidachi*.

The *uchidachi* takes one step to his rear with his right foot, followed with a sliding motion of his left foot, bringing the *kensen* of his sword under and to the right side of the *shidachi's* sword in the process (fig. 8.50*a*). The *shidachi* keeps the point of his sword at the *uchidachi's* throat and maintains control of the *uchidachi's* sword with the *shinogi* of his own sword. The *shidachi* now steps forward on his left foot, followed by his right, and makes a small thrusting motion. The *uchidachi* steps back again with his left foot, followed by his right, while bringing his sword under and to the right of the *shidachi's* sword, trying to apply pressure against the *shidachi's* sword in the process (fig. 8.50*b*) The *shidachi* takes three steps forward starting with his right foot, left foot, then right foot, all the while raising his *kensen* from the *uchidachi's* throat until it is in the middle of his face (fig. 8.50*c*). As the *shidachi* advances, the *uchidachi* takes three small steps backward, beginning on his left foot, and assumes *gedan-no-kamae*.

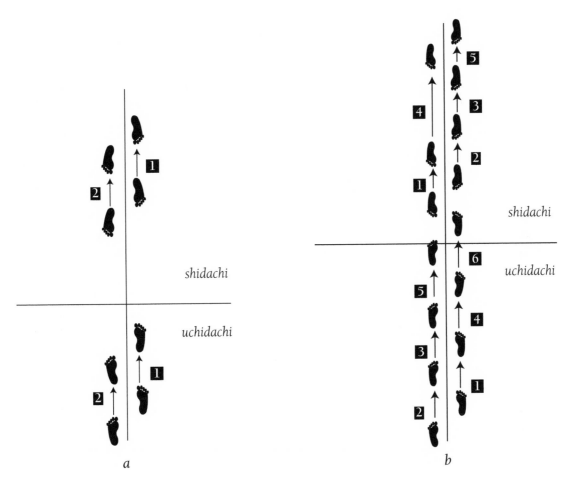

FIGURE 8.51. *Footwork for sanbonme.*

The *shidachi* steps backward with his left foot (fig. 8.51*a*, step 1); the *uchidachi* starts his *kensen* upward slowly but does not move. The *shidachi* now steps back with his right foot (step 2); the *uchidachi* continues to move his sword up but still does not move his body. This upward movement of the *uchidachi's* sword is followed by a downward movement of the *shidachi's* sword until they meet in *chudan-no-kamae*. The *shidachi* now takes three steps back starting on his left foot, then stepping with his right and then again with his left (fig. 8.51*b*). The *uchidachi* follows these movements as though being pulled by a magnetic force; right foot first, then left, then right, as in normal walking. Thus both swordsmen arrive back at their starting point, right foot forward.

a   *b*

FIGURE 8.52. *Lowering the swords in sanbonme.*

In figure 8.52*a* the *uchidachi* has started his sword downward, followed by the *shidachi,* until they arrive in low posture. When each *kensen* is even with the other's left knee, they turn the cutting edges of their swords to the left (fig. 8.52*b*).

Starting on the left (rear) foot, the *shidachi* following the *uchidachi,* each takes five small steps to the rear (fig. 8.53). They assume *chudan-no-kamae* and are ready for the next *kata.*

Sanbonme deals solely with using the *kensen* to keep the attacker physically and mentally off balance. In kendo or kenjitsu we refer to this as *mitsu-no-kujiki,* or "three ways to unbalance your opponent." The three methods are called *ken-o-korosu,* sword control; *waza-o-korosu,* technical control; and *ki-o-korosu,* mental unbalancing.

Ken-o-korosu

Ken-o-korosu is a method of pressing, sweeping, or flipping your opponent's sword to throw him off balance. When you face your opponent and his *kamae* seems to be perfect, take a

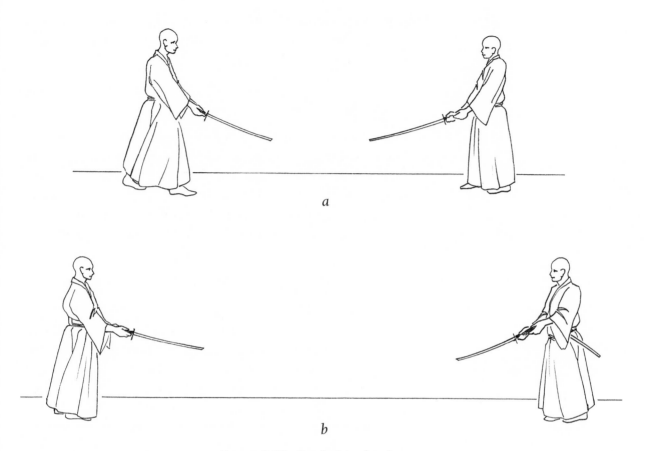

a

b

FIGURE 8.53. *Conclusion of sanbonme.*

small step forward while pressing lightly down on his sword. Keep your *kensen* in the center of his body. Whether you use the pressing, sweeping, or flipping method on your small move forward, be sure to use your entire body and not just your hands. As your opponent reacts to your movement, watch for an opportunity to attack. Be mentally and physically prepared to move on his response with your own cut or thrust. Even if you do nothing more than maintain your *kensen* in the center of his body, you will be able to control whatever action he might take by upsetting his mental stability. *Ken-o-korosu* is the most basic of all three techniques.

Waza-o-korosu

Chiba Sensei said it best: "Just be yourself. Trust in the techniques you feel you have mastered through your basic practice. They will be the ones that will determine whether you lose or win, not only in a duel but in life itself." Technical control has to start at the tip of your sword, but if your opponent is strong and manages to gain control there are two basic ways to regain control:

1. Make a rapid attack and move close. This will make it impossible for him to continue with his own technique.
2. When your opponent starts his attack, keep spoiling it with your own *kensen* control by keeping center and not moving your sword tip from side to side. This will usually frustrate him and force him to try his favorite technique prematurely, making it easy for you to spoil its effect also.

Whether in actual combat or in practicing *kendo kata*, all three methods must work together simultaneously. Always keep in mind that spoiling your opponent's technique will be impossible unless you first upset his physical posture and thereby his mental attitude.

Ki-o-korosu

Ki-o-korosu is exemplified by attacking or counterattacking with great force, using great *kiai* and spirit. This produces fright in your opponent, thereby spoiling his mental and spiritual inner strength and upsetting his mental balance. If he starts thinking about defense in the middle of his attack, you have won the advantage and your counterattack will become easy.

One cannot fully understand *ki-o-korosu* without some application of *mitsu-no-sen*, the "three *sen*" or techniques of forestalling in combat kendo. These can be broken down into three types of move: *sensen-no-sen*, *senzen-no-sen*, and *go-no-sen*.

Sensen-no-sen is used when you can see or feel your attacker's intention. It involves *debana-waza*, some of the most sophisticated *waza* in swordsmanship. Basically, a *debana-waza* involves cutting at the instant of your opponent's "movement"—which may be the thought of moving or attacking as much as a physical motion itself. This movement (or thought of movement) is the "void" all kendoists search for in their opponents. It arises after the mind has told the body to attack; it lies between the thought and the body movement.

Senzen-no-sen comprises techniques of evasion, such as *nuki-waza*. As your opponent attacks, simply step to the side at a ninety-degree angle or to the rear at a forty-five-degree angle, thereby allowing the opponent's attack to cut empty air. When his attack ends after missing his target, step forward and cut his head, wrist, or body. *Ipponme* is an example of *nuki-waza*.

Go-no-sen is delayed forestalling. When your attacker hesitates for any reason, you can use *kaeshi-waza*, or techniques of deflection; *uchi-otoshi-waza*, or techniques of striking down the opponent's sword to upset his balance; or *suriage-waza*, techniques of parrying with the right or left side of your sword (*shinogi*).

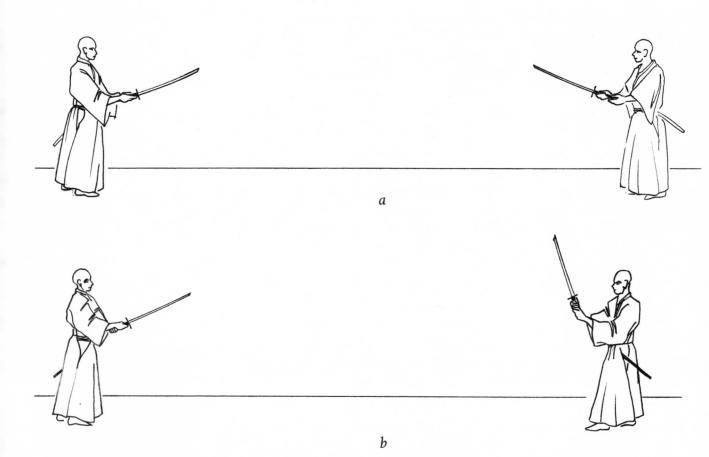

FIGURE 8.54 (*a–b*). *Opening of yonhonme.*

YONHONME

Yonhonme begins with each participant in *chudan-no-kamae*. The *uchidachi* is on the right and the *shidachi* is on the left (fig. 8.54a). The *uchidachi* starts the action by stepping forward with his left foot, taking *hasso-no-kamae* in the process (fig. 8.54b). The *shidachi*, seeing the *uchidachi* take this aggressive action,

c

d

FIGURE 8.54 (*c–d*). *Opening of yonhonme.*

follows by stepping back with his right foot and assumes *waki-no-kamae* (fig. 8.54*c*). Both the *shidachi* and the *uchidachi* are still nine steps apart and have taken their positions (fig. 8.54*d*).

Figure 8.55 shows a closer look at the *uchidachi's hasso-no-kamae.* The *shidachi* and the *uchidachi* now take three small

FIGURE 8.55. *The uchidachi's hasso-no-kamae.*

steps forward, the *uchidachi* starting the forward movement and the *shidachi* following immediately. In these three forward steps, which are smaller than the usual three steps taken in the previous *kata*, the *uchidachi* slides his left foot forward (first step), steps with his right, steps with his left, then pauses. The *shidachi* does the same, bringing both attacker and defender to a *to-ma* interval (fig. 8.56a).

As the *uchidachi* steps forward with his right (rear) foot, he simultaneously brings his sword upward to the *jodan* position and, without pause, cuts downward and to the front, trying for the center of the *shidachi's* forehead. The *shidachi* follows, at the same time stepping forward with his right foot and bringing his

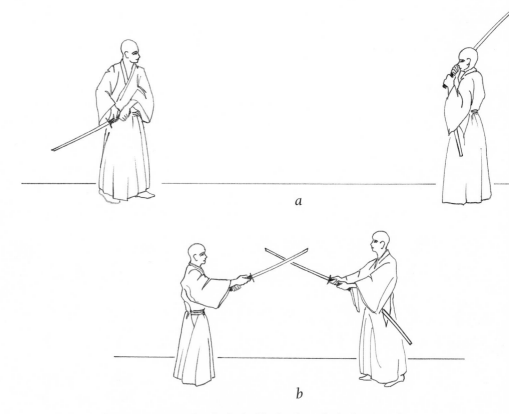

a

b

FIGURE 8.56. *The shidachi blocks the uchidachi's attack.*

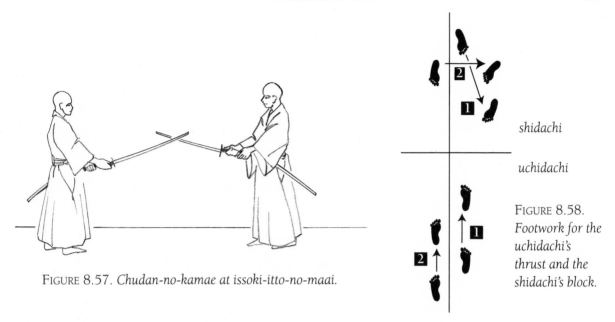

FIGURE 8.57. *Chudan-no-kamae at issoki-itto-no-maai.*

shidachi

uchidachi

FIGURE 8.58.
Footwork for the uchidachi's thrust and the shidachi's block.

sword from w*aki-no-kamae* to *jodan*; he does not stop in *jodan* but meets the *uchidachi's* sword on the left side and halts the *uchidachi's* first attack (fig. 8.56*b*). The two swords should strike each other using the first six inches of the blade with *shinogi* touching.

The *shidachi* and the *uchidachi* lower their swords to *chudan-no-kamae* and are now in *issoku-itto-no-maai*, or the one-step cutting interval (fig. 8.57). The *uchidachi* feels a chance to attack. He turns the blade slightly to his right (counterclockwise), slides forward with his right foot followed immediately by his left (but keeping it behind his right), delivers a two-handed thrust to the *shidachi's* so-

FIGURE 8.59. *The shidachi's block, with detail of sword position.*

lar plexus, and shouts "*Yah!*" The *shidachi* advances his left foot diagonally to his left (see fig. 8.58 for footwork) while simultaneously lifting his hands upward and keeping a firm but slightly loose grip on the *tsuka*, and blocks the *uchidachi's* thrust with the *shinogi* of the left side of his sword (fig. 8.59*a*; fig. 8.59*b* shows sword position).

The *shidachi* brings his sword up and over his head and delivers a cut to the *uchidachi's* forehead with the first six inches of his sword (while drawing his right foot to a position behind his left) and *kiais* "*Toh!*" (fig. 8.60). He should hold this cut long enough to have a good *zanshin*.

The *uchidachi* now starts the next action after the *shidachi's* *zanshin* by stepping back with his rear (left) foot and assuming *chudan-no-kamae* (fig. 8.61*a*). The *shidachi* follows by stepping

FIGURE 8.60. *The shidachi delivers a cut to the uchidachi's forehead.*

back to his right with his right foot followed by his left and assuming *chudan-no-kamae*. They are now in *issoku-itto-no-maai* (fig. 8.61*b*). In figure 8.61*c* the *uchidachi*, followed by the *shidachi*, has lowered his sword to a low posture. When their *kensen* are about even with the other's left knee, they turn the cutting edges of the swords to their left (clockwise) (fig. 8.61*d*).

a

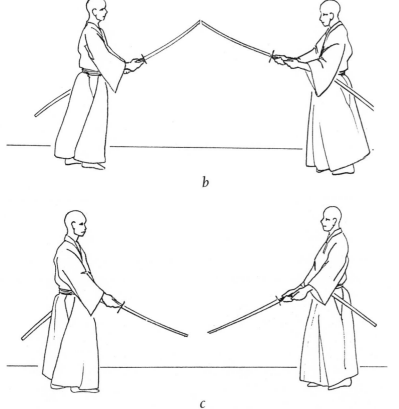

b

c

d

FIGURE 8.61 (*a–d*). *Conclusion of yonhonme.*

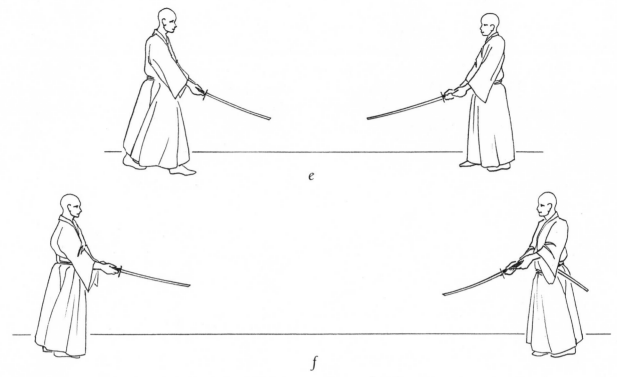

e

f

FIGURE 8.61 (*e–f*). *Conclusion of yonhonme.*

Starting on the left (rear) foot, the *uchidachi*, followed by the
shidachi, takes five small or normal steps to the rear (figs. 8.61*e*
and *f*). The *shidachi* and the *uchidachi* have assumed *chudan-no-
kamae* and are now ready for the next *kata*.

GOHONME

In figure 8.62*a* the *uchidachi* is on the right and the *shidachi* is
on the left in the beginning posture of *chudan-no-kamae*. In figures 8.62*b* and *c* the *uchidachi* steps forward with his left (rear)
foot and assumes the left *jodan-no-kamae* posture. In figure
8.62*c* the *shidachi* responds to the *uchidachi*'s aggressive action
by raising his *kensen* up and forward. The *shidachi* turns his

FIGURE 8.64. *Suriage-waza.*

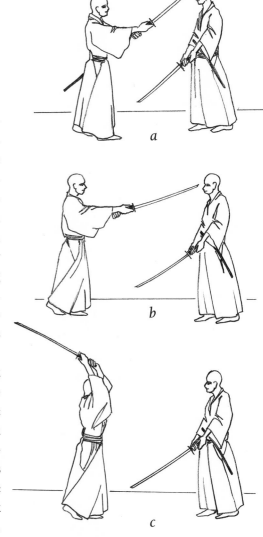

FIGURE 8.65. *The shidachi's cut to the uchidachi's shomen.*

then lowers his sword. This blocking movement, called *suriage-waza*, or rising sliding technique, demands a high degree of accuracy. It requires that you use an upward sliding parry with the side of your sword against the side of the sword of your opponent, who has started his own downward cutting action. In using *suriage-waza*, you must coordinate your movements with the direction of the attacker's sword and the lack of stability in his posture. The upward slide and swinging of your sword over your head must be performed in a unbroken series and using your wrist to turn the edge of your sword slightly to the right. While you're stepping backward, never allow your heels to touch the floor and keep your back straight. You should always have the feeling of going forward to meet your attacker.

In figure 8.65a the *shidachi* slides forward with his right foot followed by his left (but not passing the right), delivers a cut to the center of the *uchidachi's* head or *shomen*, stopping about one inch from the forehead, and yells "*Toh!*" The *uchidachi*, on missing his target and on the *shidachi's* forward movement, continues lowering his sword. In figure 8.65b the *shidachi* starts his *zanshin* by lowering his *kensen* to the *uchidachi's* eyes. He pauses slightly and then steps back with his right (front) foot and takes a *jodan-no-kamae* with the left foot forward (fig. 8.65c). These movements should flow smoothly.

After a short pause, the *uchidachi* starts his sword upward.

The *shidachi* follows the *uchidachi's* movement by stepping back with his left (front) foot. Each person moves his sword upward and downward until they meet in the *chudan-no-kamae* (fig. 8.66a). The *uchidachi* take three steps backward, the *shidachi* three steps forward. The *uchidachi* starts the action with his left (rear) foot, then steps with his right and then his left. The *shidachi* starts forward by sliding his right foot first, then his left, and then his right. This moment returns them to their starting position. These three steps are done while remaining in *chudan-no-kamae*. The first two inches of the swords remain crossed. In figure 8.66b the *uchidachi* starts the downward action with his sword, followed by the *shidachi*, both stopping at a level even with the other's left (rear) knee and turning the cutting edges of their swords slightly to the left (clockwise) in the process (fig. 8.66c).

In figure 8.67a the *uchidachi* starts the action by stepping to his rear, left foot, right foot, left foot. The *shidachi* follows to his rear, left foot, right foot, left foot (fig. 8.67b). With their right feet forward they are now again nine steps apart (fig. 8.67c). The *uchidachi* and the *shidachi* now take the *chudan-no-kamae* and are ready to start the next *kata*.

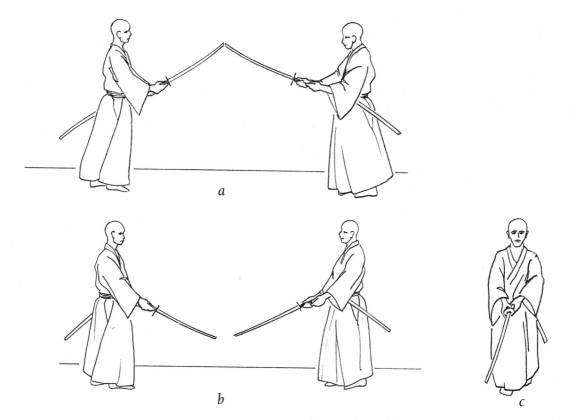

a

b

c

FIGURE 8.66. *Lowering the swords in gohonme.*

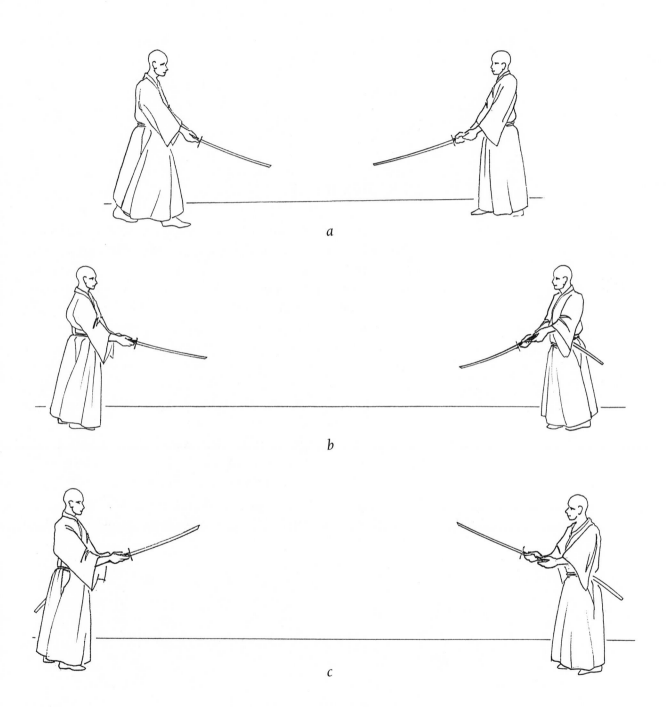

a

b

c

FIGURE 8.67. *Conclusion of gohonme.*

ROPPONME

The *uchidachi* and *shidachi* start *ropponme* in the *chudan-no-kamae*. The *shidachi,* on the left, starts the action by lowering his sword to *gedan-no-kamae* while the *uchidachi* stays in *chudan-no-kamae*. They are nine steps apart (fig. 8.68*a*). Beginning on the right (forward) foot, each takes three steps forward, right foot sliding forward first, then left, then right, meeting in the center at the *issoku-itto-no-maai* (fig. 8.68*b*). The *shidachi,* feeling a weakness in the *uchidachi's kamae,* or spirit, starts the action by raising his *kensen* to *chudan-no-kamae*. The *uchidachi* tries to control the tip of the *shidachi's* sword from above but the *shidachi's kamae* is too strong. The *uchidachi* sees the *shidachi's* sword moving upward and turns his sword edge about ten degrees to his right (counterclockwise), trying to hold down the *shidachi's* sword. They do not touch. Because the *shidachi* does not move, the *uchidachi* gets a feeling that the *shidachi* might thrust his sword into his chest. Therefore, the *uchidachi* must retreat (fig. 8.68*c*).

FIGURE 8.68. *Opening of ropponme.*

FIGURE 8.69. *The shidachi raises his kensen.*

a

b

FIGURE 8.70. *The uchidachi's cut to the shidachi's right kote.*

The *uchidachi* steps back with his right foot, taking a left *jodan-no-kamae*. The *shidachi* reacts by sliding forward with his right foot followed by his left but not passing the right. Simultaneously, he raises his *kensen* to point at the *uchidachi's* left forearm (fig. 8.69a). In figure 8.69b the *uchidachi*, seeing that there is no advantage in this posture, steps back with his left (front) foot and assumes the *chudan-no-kamae* once more. The *shidachi* returns to a regular *chudan-no-kamae* while again sliding slightly forward with his right foot followed by his left (but not passing the right). The *shidachi* and the *uchidachi* are now once again in the *issoku-itto-no-maai*.

In figure 8.70 the *uchidachi* senses a weakness in the *shidachi's* defense, slides forward with his right foot followed by his left (but not passing the right), and cuts the right wrist or *kote* of the *shidachi*. The *shidachi* feels the attack coming and, as the *uchidachi* moves forward, slides his left foot back diagonally to his left followed by his right. See figure 8.71 for footwork.

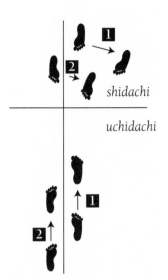

As the *uchidachi's* cut is being delivered, the *shidachi* uses the *shinogi* of the right side of his sword to deflect the *uchidachi's* cut. He then slides forward on his right foot followed by his left (but not passing the right) and, staying on the same angle (as in fig 8.71), delivers a cut to the *uchidachi's* right wrist (fig. 8.72). They maintain eye contact, and the *uchidachi* turns his head to the right very slightly. The *uchidachi* now lowers his *kensen* and steps back one step diagonally to the left with the left foot first then his right, but not passing the left.

FIGURE 8.71. *Footwork for the uchidachi's cut to the shidachi's right kote.*

FIGURE 8.72. *The shidachi's cut to the uchidachi's right kote.*

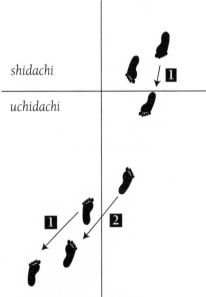

FIGURE 8.73. *Footwork for the shidachi's cut to the uchidachi's right kote.*

As the *uchidachi* makes this move, the *shidachi* smoothly but quickly advances his left (rear) foot and assumes the left *jodan-no-kamae* (figs. 8.73 and 8.74*a*). In figure 8.74*b* the *shidachi* has not relaxed his physical or mental feeling and maintains *zanshin*. The *shidachi* now moves his right foot back to the original line and retracts his left foot slightly behind his right foot as the *uchidachi* starts his *kensen* upward. The *uchidachi* takes one step to his right with his right foot followed by his left; the participants are now in their original positions (fig. 8.74*c*).

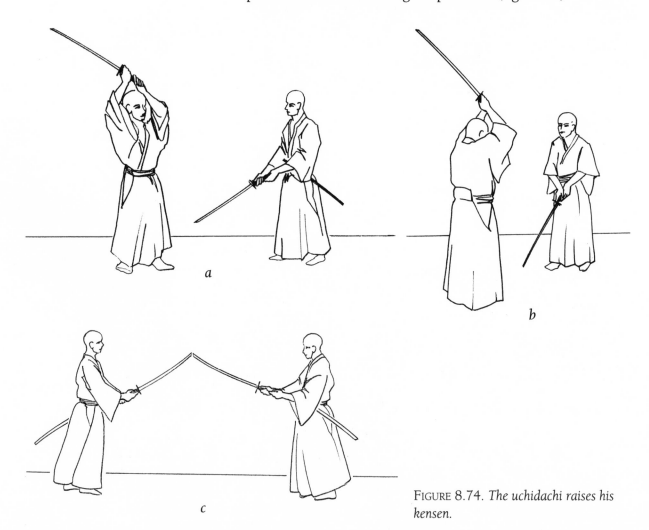

FIGURE 8.74. *The uchidachi raises his kensen.*

The *shidachi* lowers his *kensen* until they both meet in *chudan-no-kamae*. In figure 8.75*a* both the *uchidachi* and the *shidachi* lower their *kensen* so that they point to the other's left (rear) knee. They then turn the edges of their swords slightly to the left (clockwise) (fig. 8.75*b*). In figure 8.75*c* the *uchidachi* starts the action by stepping to the rear with his left foot. The *shidachi* follows, and each takes five normal steps to the rear (fig. 8.75*d*). They are now in their original position, nine steps apart, and assume *chudan-no-kamae* (fig. 8.75*e*). They are ready for the next *kata*.

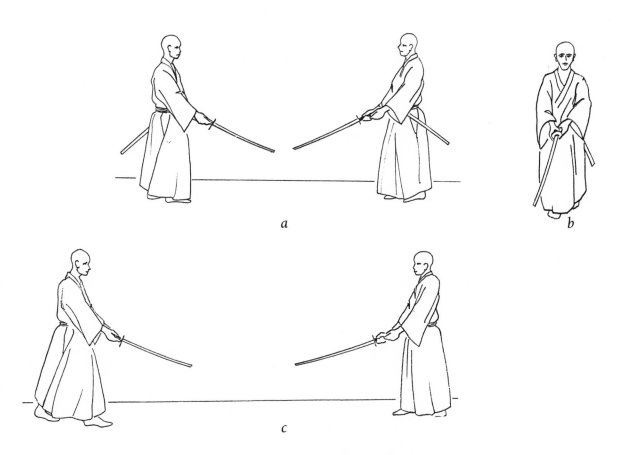

a

b

c

FIGURE 8.75 (*a–c*). *Conclusion of ropponme.*

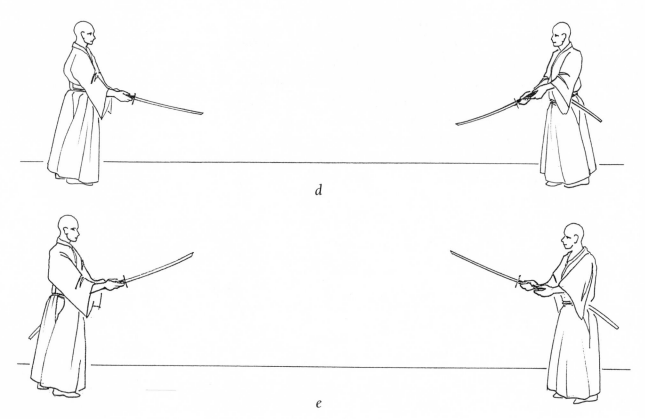

d

e

FIGURE 8.75 (*d–e*). *Conclusion of ropponme.*

NANAHONME

Nanahonme is the last long sword form in the All Japan Kendo Federation *kata*. It begins with the *uchidachi* on the right and the *shidachi* on the left as at the end of *ropponme*: nine steps apart and in *chudan-no-kamae*, right foot forward. The *uchidachi* starts the action, followed by the *shidachi*. Both take three

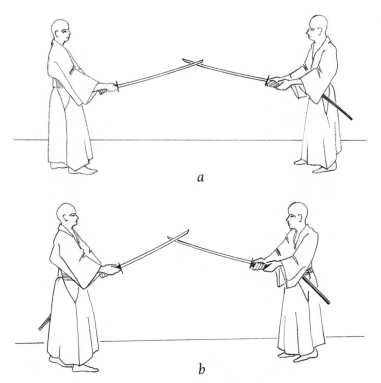

a

b

FIGURE 8.76. *Opening of nanahonme.*

steps forward by sliding the right foot forward first, then stepping with the left, then the right, coming to the position shown
in figure 8.76*a*; the first two or three inches of their swords
cross. The *uchidachi*, feeling a weakness in the *shidachi's* defense, turns the edge of his sword slightly to the right and
points his *kensen* at the *shidachi's* solar plexus (fig. 8.76*b*). Using the *shinogi* of the left side of his sword on the left side of the
shidachi's sword, the *uchidachi* slides his sword forward and
slightly upward using both hands while taking a sliding step
forward with his right (front) foot about three or four inches.
The *shidachi* responds by pushing upward against the *uchidachi's* sword with his own sword while taking a small step
backward two or three inches with his left (rear) foot. Both then

FIGURE 8.77. *The uchidachi's cut to the shidachi's shomen.*

FIGURE 8.78. *Footwork for the uchidachi's cut to the shidachi's shomen.*

step back to their original positions. Consequently, both the *uchidachi* and the *shidachi* bring their *kensen* slightly upward, pushing forward with their hands and hips, and then quickly retreat to their starting point and assume the *chudan-no-kamae*.

The *uchidachi*, now feeling he has a small advantage by mentally off-balancing the *shidachi*, steps forward with his left (rear) foot and brings his sword upward to the *jodan-no-kamae* position. Not pausing, he steps forward with his right foot and delivers a cut to the *shidachi's* forehead (*shomen*) and kiais "Yah!" The *shidachi* senses the attack and, as the *uchidachi's* sword starts its upward path, slides his right foot forward and slightly diagonally to the right while bringing his sword to his left side (see fig. 8.77 and footwork in fig. 8.78).

a *b*

FIGURE 8.79. *The shidachi's right do cut.*

In figure 8.79*a* the *shidachi* has stepped diagonally to his right again, this time with his left foot, and begun his right body (*do*) cut; he *kiais* "*Toh!*" See figure 8.79*b* for the position of the sword against the *uchidachi*. The footwork is shown in figure 8.78.

The *shidachi* now follows through with his cut, stepping forward once more with his right foot and extending both arms straight out to his right side at shoulder level. The cutting edge of the sword is facing away from the *uchidachi*. On the last step with his right foot, he kneels down on his right knee. His left knee is raised. He then pivots to his left so he is facing the *uchidachi* (fig. 8.80*a*). Nothing but the ball of the right foot and right knee are touching the floor, as seen in the footwork in figure 8.78.

FIGURE 8.80 (*a*). *The shidachi kneels, turns, and takes jodan-no-kamae.*

a

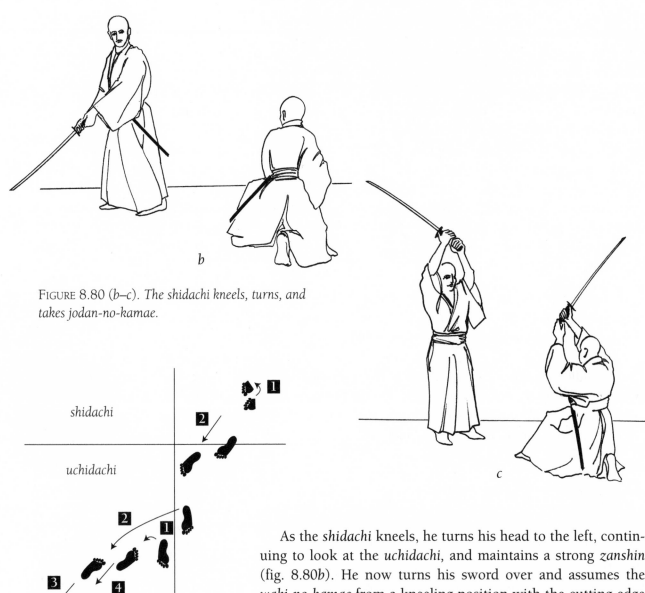

FIGURE 8.80 (*b–c*). *The shidachi kneels, turns, and takes jodan-no-kamae.*

FIGURE 8.81. *Footwork for the shidachi's turn and the uchidachi's response.*

As the *shidachi* kneels, he turns his head to the left, continuing to look at the *uchidachi*, and maintains a strong *zanshin* (fig. 8.80*b*). He now turns his sword over and assumes the *waki-no-kamae* from a kneeling position with the cutting edge away from him and his *kensen* pointed slightly downward and to the rear. The *uchidachi* has turned his head to his left, trying to keep eye contact with the *shidachi*. After a brief pause, the *uchidachi* turns his body to face the *shidachi* by pivoting on the balls of his feet. The *uchidachi* assumes only momentarily the *jodan-no-kamae* posture. The *shidachi* responds by sliding his right foot to the right so it will align with his raised left knee. The *shidachi* now also takes the *jodan-no-kamae* posture but from a kneeling position while remaining in *zanshin*. In other words, the *shidachi* makes it clear to the *uchidachi* that he is still on his guard (see fig. 8.80*c* and footwork in fig. 8.81).

In figure 8.82 the *uchidachi* has assumed the *chudan-no-kamae* posture without moving his feet. The *shidachi* responds simultaneously with a kneeling *chudan-no-kamae* posture. Their swords may or may not be crossed. If the swords are crossed they should be so for no more than one inch. If they are not crossed they should be no more than one-half inch apart.

The next part is most important. The *shidachi* moves first by pushing forward and upward with his rear foot to a standing position while maintaining the *chudan-no-kamae*. From a standing position, the *shidachi* steps forward with his right foot. The *uchidachi* responds by moving one step to his rear with his left foot (fig. 8.83; refer back to fig. 8.81 for footwork). It is important for the *uchidachi* to be in the same rhythm as the *shidachi* as he rises from his kneeling position and steps forward in one continuous movement.

FIGURE 8.82. *Standing and kneeling chudan-no-kamae.*

FIGURE 8.83. *The shidachi rises and steps forward.*

FIGURE 8.84. *Sonkyu and sword return.*

FIGURE 8.85. *Detail of sonkyu and sword return.*

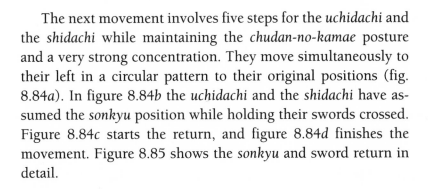

The next movement involves five steps for the *uchidachi* and the *shidachi* while maintaining the *chudan-no-kamae* posture and a very strong concentration. They move simultaneously to their left in a circular pattern to their original positions (fig. 8.84*a*). In figure 8.84*b* the *uchidachi* and the *shidachi* have assumed the *sonkyu* position while holding their swords crossed. Figure 8.84*c* starts the return, and figure 8.84*d* finishes the movement. Figure 8.85 shows the *sonkyu* and sword return in detail.

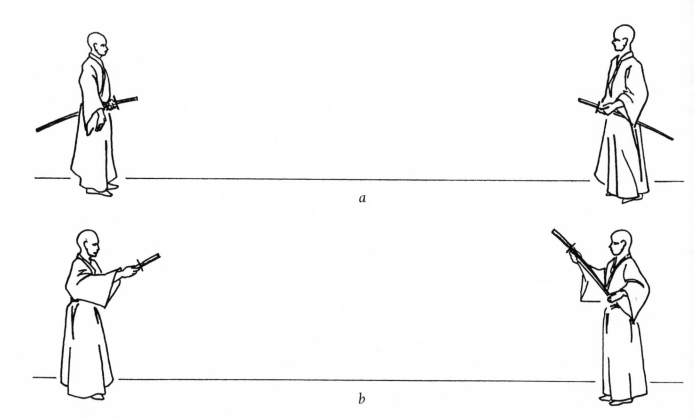

a

b

FIGURE 8.86. *Returning to opening position and removing the sword from the obi.*

c

After returning the swords to their *saya*, the *uchidachi* and *shidachi* rise but still maintain a strong feeling of alertness. The *uchidachi* starts the next action by moving first. Each takes five steps backward starting with the left foot. They arrive at their starting point nine steps apart (fig. 8.86*a*). The left thumb is on the *tsuba* and the right hand is to the side. The *uchidachi*, followed by the *shidachi*, removes the sword from his *obi* (fig. 8.86*b*). Figure 8.86*c* is a front view of this movement.

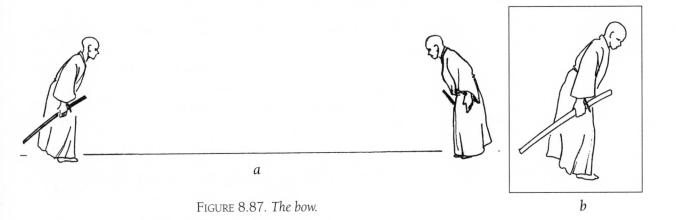

FIGURE 8.87. *The bow.*

With the sword now in the right hand and the thumb on the *tsuba*, cutting edge up, each bows; their left hands stay at a natural position at the side (see fig. 8.87*a* and detail in fig. 8.87*b*).

The *uchidachi* now takes *sonkyu* while bringing his sword to his waist. The *shidachi* then steps back with his right foot, followed by his left, to where he has placed his *kodachi* (figs. 8.88 and 8.89).

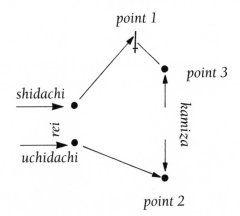

FIGURE 8.88. *Diagram of movements in nanahonme.*

FIGURE 8.89. *The shidachi returns to his kodachi.*

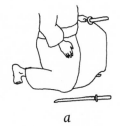

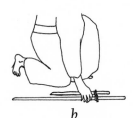

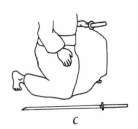

a

b

c

FIGURE 8.90.
*The shidachi lays down
the katana and picks up
the kodachi.*

Figure 8.90*a* shows the *shidachi* in a kneeling position. In figure 8.90*b* he has laid down the *katana* to the outside of the *kodachi*. In figure 8.90*c* he has picked up the *kodachi* with his right hand and passed it to his left side. He is now ready to start the three remaining *kata* of the All Japan Kendo Federation with the short sword.

❖

It seems as though I have just started writing this book and here we are at the end. I would like to leave the reader with this thought: Youth and beauty are forever the same. Those who wish to be old were born old. Kendo is for everyone, so enjoy it and try to stay on the true path. As Chiba Sensei would say,

May you live forever,
And may I never die.

APPENDIX

THE GOSHI, OR "COUNTRY SAMURAI"

The following excerpts are quoted from the brochure
Soldier and Peasant in Japan: The Origins of Conscription,
written by E. Herbert Norman and published in 1943 by the
Institute of Pacific Relations. In the interest of space,
all footnote references and footnotes
have been intentionally deleted.

THE GOSHI

The *locus classicus* where the origin and social status of the *goshi* are most authoritatively described is found in Volume 4 of the *Jikata Hanrei Roku*. The passage in question reads: In early times the division of *hyakusho* and *samurai* was unknown; all were farmers (*nofu*). During the wars the strong farmers went to fight, and the weaker ones remained to till the land. Finally, between 1321 and 1334, the commencement of the Ashikaga period, when the greatest internal confusion existed, the separation between the farmer class and the *samurai* class occurred. From this time *goshi* and *samurai* formed the sword-bearing class. Thus the *goshi* of today represent the source from which farmers and *samurai* alike sprang. The *goshi*, however, did not become warriors and receive an income from a territorial land. They owned and cultivated their own lands. They were not subject to military service, except for the defense of the province. They differed on the other hand from ordinary farmers, and were quite above them in rank. The *goshi* had the privilege which distinguished the upper classes of being addressed in public by his family name. The family of Iyeyasu was of *goshi* descent. He was the eighth in line of an adopted son of Matsudaira Tarozayemon, a *goshi* of Mikawa. The family of Satsuma and, in fact, those of most *daimyo* were of *goshi* origin.

A further comment on the *goshi* made by the American legal student of Japanese land tenure, the late Dr. Wigmore, reads as follows: "As a class existing under Tokugawa rule, they probably represented those larger landowners and minor territorial lords who did not take part in the wars attending the rise of the Tokugawa, and on submitting were left in possession of their land."

". . . A farmer well off was sometimes rewarded by the Tokugawa Government, for services rendered, by the title and rank of *goshi*. The record or time was always kept in the office of the *daikan*. This differed from the bestowal of *samurai* rank, e.g., for charitable action in times of distress, repairing a dike, etc. Rich men, in hopes of receiving this honor, often performed such work. The title was for life only, not hereditary, as that of *goshi* was, and the technical name was *Ichidai taito-gomen* (one-life-wear-sword-permission)."

". . . After the Restoration of 1867, the estates of the feudal nobility were confiscated and the titles abolished. The *goshi*, however, retained their land, though they lost their titles."

Goshi are to be distinguished from the *go-zamurai* or the *inaka-samurai*. Although they were of the same origin as *goshi*, their development was different. *Go-zamurai* and *inaka-samurai* were true *samurai* who rendered military service to a lord, but they did not live in the residence of their lord nor in the castle-town of the fief. They were thus the intermediate between the ordinary *samurai* and the *goshi*, being rather more independent and rustic than the ordinary castle-town *samurai* but definitely inferior in status to the castle-town *samurai*. But since they were true *samurai* they had the right, which the *goshi* did not, of bestowing upon their retainers permission to wear two swords.

THE GOSHI OF TOSA

Tosa was a clan where *goshi* existed in considerable numbers and enjoyed a rather favored position in society right down to the time of the Restoration.

After the separation of *nohei* in Tosa, those families who were of gentle birth had to be regulated by the ruling Chosok-abe family in such a way as to mark their superiority to the peasantry. Under the rule of Tadayoshi, who succeeded to the fief in 1605, the administration of the clan was drastically re-formed. In order to tighten local administration, he bestowed the rank of *samurai* on families who had long served in an of-ficial capacity, giving them small estates. These became *goshi* and were placed in charge of village administration, and their chief task was the pacification of the peasantry. Their function was thus control over the lower classes in the interests of the feudal authorities. This social reform took place in the eigh-teenth year of Keicho (1613) and so those promoted to *samu-rai* or *goshi* rank were known as Keicho *goshi*.

This was the oldest type of *goshi* in Tosa, who became the village aristocracy; and these *goshi* were often interchangeable or identical with the *shoya* (village headman).

Thus the first recorded appearance of *goshi* in Tosa marked a trend toward appointing as local officials men of some social consideration or military merit. We have recorded in an ancient record of Tosa the following observa-tion: "In ancient times, sometimes the *shoya* came from the *goshi* and sometimes the *goshi* became *shoya* and each set up a separate house or again those attached to the *goshi* labored in the yakuba (*shoya*'s official residence, or village administration office); sometimes *goshi* and *shoya* were distinct terms, sometimes they overlapped and again they were mutually interchangeable."

The next type of *goshi* in Tosa appears after the annihilation of the Chosokabe family, which had championed the cause of Hideyoshi's son Hideyori against Ieyasu in the Osaka campaign of 1614–15. The fief of Tosa passed into the hands of a Tokugawa ally, the Yamanouchi family, and the retainers of the Chosokabe became *ronin*. However, the famous clan administrator, Nonaka Kenzan (1616–64), feared to have within the clan precincts so many declassed and embittered *samurai* whose complaints and intrigues among the peasants might have serious consequences for the newly established Yamanouchi rule. Therefore, he made it his policy to give these Chosokabe retainers, who still remained in Tosa, virgin land to be opened up. Once this land was reclaimed it became *ryochi* or fief land and those working it were to enjoy certain privileges. This plan was first commenced in the first and second years of Shoto (1684–5). About one hundred families took advantage of it and became known as *hyaku-shu goshi*.

This category of *hyaku-shu goshi* was of a restricted nature so that after fifty years of Yamanouchi rule, in order to obliterate the bitter memories which might survive among the defeated Chosokabe retainers, a further opening up of the *goshi* system was effected. Those who applied to the clan government were given permission to reclaim wild land and in return were given the rank of *goshi*. At the time when this further encouragement of *goshi* status was given to those households which desired to reclaim land, some two hundred families took advantage of the opportunity, and this new class of *goshi* became known as *hyakunin-shu nami goshi*.

As time went on, the number of those who reclaimed land and were given the rank of *goshi* was steadily increased so that by the year 1747 there were listed in Tosa 794 families of *goshi* rank, and they held a social position so strong that it could not lightly be ignored. These *goshi* were virtually *samurai* in social status and so definitely above *yonin*, or lower-class retainer, possessing as they did the right of having a surname and wearing a sword. They also enjoyed the privilege of being interviewed in the *Tochaku no Ma* (one of the outer chambers in the clan palace); they participated in certain ceremonial privileges and shared with *samurai* the honor of jousting on horseback in the presence of the lord, so that their social position was far from mean or lowly. After the reforms of Nonaka Kenzan, it was possible even for the *goshi* of Tosa to become formally accepted as true retainers of the lord and their holdings thus became *chigyo* (benefice or small fief) and such *goshi* were known as *tozama goshi*. But this rank was only conferred on a few, and in general most of the *Tosa goshi* remained inferior in status to the castle-town *samurai*. In fact, we find in the clan records the following instructions addressed to *goshi* and *goyonin* (lower-class clan retainers): "Whenever you meet a *samurai*, you must remove your hat and show reverence as far as possible and not be impolite." *Goshi* were also prohibited from building a villa, and when walking in the castle-town they were not permitted to wear *bokuri* (wooden clogs) or to carry a *higasa* (parasol) or to don a *zukin* (wimple or hood) as might most of the townsmen. This is a classic example in feudal Japan of the minute differentiation within each class and division of class by ceremonial privileges and sumptuary gradation, used to emphasize the social inferiority of the rustic *goshi* to the city *samurai* and well-to-do burghers.

With the insatiable land-hunger of feudalism as a driving force, the number of those willing to reclaim land under contract (*ukeoi*) with the clan authorities, in return for the acquisition of *goshi* status, steadily increased. This increase tended to cheapen the rank of *goshi*, and many wealthy peasants and *chonin* entered the ranks of *goshi* in order to acquire *bushi* status. Not only in Tosa but in other clans this was an opening in the solid wall of Tokugawa class hierarchy through which wealthy and socially ambitious peasants or *chonin* could become *samurai*.

In the fifth year of Bunsei (1822), a document of the Tosa clan reads in part as follows: "If those who do not wear swords are permitted to open land, on that day they are granted the right to take a name and wear a sword (*myoji taito gomen*); if they open land which yields as much as fifteen *koku*, they are allowed to become *goshi*."

These *goshi* who went to swell the ranks of lower officials were very active in village administration at the close of the Tokugawa period. In many of the volunteer bands which fought the Bakufu armies on the eve of the Restoration, *goshi* often played a leading part.

COMPARISON OF GOSHI WITH ENGLISH COUNTERPARTS

Analogies between Japanese and European feudal society are dangerous and distorting if applied rigidly. But sometimes an attempt at comparing, even if roughly, some obscure Japanese feudal institution or practice with a European parallel or equivalent may help to throw a ray of light on the lesser known Japanese counterpart.

In the foregoing discussion of *goshi*, we noticed that this generic term covered a wide variety of feudal gentry whose social position lay between the dominant *daimyo-samurai* class, that is, the ruling class, on the one hand and the peasantry on the other, but definitely closer to the former, enjoying many of its rights and privileges and sharing its outlook and prejudices. The position of the *goshi* differed according to clan and era. We have already compared the *goshi* to the Tudor Justices of the Peace, but this analogy is not altogether happy since strictly speaking these Tudor officials were living in a society where feudalism had practically disappeared, whereas the *goshi* which we have described were an integral part of a still dominant feudalism. Accordingly, in searching for something comparable to the Japanese *goshi*, we had better look earlier in the history of feudalism in England.

If we think of the *goshi* of Satsuma, for instance, where they enjoyed long and uninterrupted authority under the *tojo* system, wherein they supervised local justice under the deputy agent of the clan government in Ka*gosh*ima, then a rough parallel in early English feudalism can be found. Both in their social position, their class outlook (i.e., as local officials who held power over the peasantry), and particularly in their administrative functions, they remind one of that somewhat mysterious and elusive body of men, referred to by Henry de Bracton in his "*De Legibus et Consuetudinibus Angliae*" as *buzones*. According to an illuminating article by Mr. Gaillard Lapsley of Trinity College, Cambridge, the *buzones* were men, who, though obscure in terms of national politics, were weighty and influential in local affairs. They were active in the county courts, particularly as doomsmen, and they also undertook the duties of a volunteer police force within the county. They flourished in the 12th and 13th centuries as an agrarian middle class, none of whom were tenants-in-chief but who were most probably respectable owners of small manors. They were the spokesmen of local public opinion, who made themselves busy, if not officious, in the affairs of the county, and the Angevin policy of local self-agency lent them an authority which made them a force not to be despised. In a later period men of this social class and administrative function would be called, first, Keepers of the Peace, and finally, in a still later age, Justices of the Peace.

Another analogy to the Japanese *goshi*, more particularly of Tosa, where the social position of *goshi* and their political role in the fief administration was somewhat higher than in other clans, may be found in the *bachilarii*. This class was the most important element in the army of Simon de Montfort, which defeated and captured Henry III at the battle of Lewes (1265). The *bachilarii* are credited with supplying political ideas to Simon, particularly in connection with the famous parliament he called in which, for the first time, two knights representing the county were summoned to aid in the collective negotiation of county business. They were most active in the courts of the hundred and county.

The *bachilarii* were apparently a homogeneous and well-knit community of middle-class feudatories, the retainers of powerful feudal lords, whose arrogance and political autocracy they feared. They naturally would support any leader who promised to weight the scale of government more heavily in favor of this *petite noblesse.*

A leading Japanese agrarian historian, Ono Takeo, has compared the *goshi* to the English yeoman. This comparison does not seem to me to be altogether illuminating since the *goshi* enjoyed a more easily definable social position; they were members, however humble, of the dominant *samurai* class, and their duties and functions can be described, given the time and territory, with almost legal precision. The position of the yeomanry, on the other hand, cannot be defined with such nicety. Their origins, moreover, were plebeian, whereas the *goshi* were mostly descendants of the aristocratic sword-bearing class. The *goshi* enjoyed many of the privileges of the ruling feudal class but the yeoman came very close to being an independent cultivator, or to be more precise, a copy-holder, whose decline, socially and economically, first became noticeable in the period of the enclosures during the Tudor era. Neither serf nor villein, the yeoman was not, on the other hand, an important element in the dominant squirearchy as was the *goshi.*

CONCLUSION

The purpose of this appendix was simply to amplify the account given in the foregoing pages where too much detail and historical analogy seemed out of place. However, the fact that a few further details have been added here does not in any way make of the appendix a full or adequate account of the subject. For anyone interested in the social history of Japan, and particularly in making an inquiry into the history of local institutions (which, if it is to be rescued from becoming a mere enumeration of offices and functions, must describe and differentiate the human material that worked the administrative machinery), a full-length study of the *goshi* should prove of value. In any account of the social stratification of Tokugawa Japan, and particularly of peasant-*samurai* relations, a discussion of the history and status of the *goshi* would be necessary. However, it would require at least a monograph to do this subject full justice, and it would entail considerable research, as the source material is scattered far and wide through the local and clan histories. This fact alone would make sweeping generalizations about the *goshi* dangerous, especially since, as it has been pointed out above, their original role and status differed widely according to locality and time.

One feature of the *goshi* that has not been mentioned but ought perhaps to be pointed out is that they were found only in the most ancient parts of Japan, i.e., Kyushu, Shikoku, and the southwestern part of Honshu. Practically no records of *goshi* in either the Kwanto or the Tohoku districts are to be found in contemporary source material. One exception to this is the case of Shinano, where *goshi* are mentioned at least in Tokugawa times.

For the purpose of the description of the *goshi* that has appeared in these pages, the general references have been, in addition to the long quotation from the *Jikata Hanrei Roku*, the standard work on the *goshi* by the well-known agrarian expert and historian, Ono Takeo, *Goshi Seido no Kenkyu* (A Study of the *Goshi* System), Tokyo, 1925; a work by the same author that gives considerable material on the social and political work of the *goshi*, *Nihon Heino Sharon* (An Historical Discussion of

Soldier Peasants in Japan), Tokyo, 1938; and finally, with particular reference to the history of the Tosa *goshi*, a work by Matsuyoshi Sadao, *Shinden no Kenkyu* (A Study of Reclaimed Land), Tokyo, 1936. All of these works have been cited within the text of this brochure. A succinct and authoritative summary of the position of *goshi* is to be found in a work not cited herein, but which, for the sake of convenience, might be mentioned, Kurita Genji: *Edo Jidai Shi* (A History of the Edo Era) in *Sogo Nihon Shi Taikei* (A Synthesis of Japanese History in Outline), Vol. XVIII, Revised Edition, Tokyo, 1939, p. 687f.

GLOSSARY

ai-uchi The situation in which both players score valid strikes simultaneously. During a match, neither strike is considered valid; they cancel each other out.

ashi Foot or feet.

ashi-sabaki Footwork used when attacking or evading; the four types are *ayumi-ashi, okuri-ashi, hiraki-ashi,* and *tsugi-ashi.*

ayumi-ashi A method of *ashi-sabaki* used to move far and quickly in the forward and backward direction; it uses ordinary walking movements made with *suri-ashi* (dragging feet).

bogu The protective armor, or gear, used in kendo, including the *men, kote, do,* and *tare* (hip and thigh protector); also called the *kendo-gu.*

bokuto A sword made of wood such as that of the oak or Japanese medlar tree; also called *boken* or *kidachi.*

budo The martial way; the unwritten code of laws governing the lives and conduct of the samurai; the precepts of samurai; chivalry.

bujutsu Literally, "martial arts." Includes forms such as *jujitsu* and *kenjitsu.*

chikai-maai The state of being closer to the opponent than *issoku-itto-maai.* Also called *chika-ma.*

chudan-no-kamae A stance where the right foot is slightly forward from an upright posture and the left foot is placed along the line of the right knee; the *shinai* is held with the right hand just below the *tsuba,* the left hand at the *tsuka gashira* (end of the *shinai* handle), and the extension of the *kensen* pointed in the range between the opponent's throat and eyebrows; the most basic stance in kendo, suitable for both offense and defense.

dan A rank indicative of one's level of skill; in kendo there are ten levels, from *shodan* to *judan.*

datotsu Striking and thrusting.

debana The moment when an opponent tries to come forward to strike or attack.

debana-waza A *waza* where one strikes into the opponent just as he is beginning a strike or attack.

do The piece of kendo equipment that covers the chest and stomach areas; a type of *waza* in which one strikes the opponent's trunk area.

fudoshin An emotional state that is unmoved by anything; also, a flexible mind that is able to respond to various changing situations.

gedan-no-kamae The stance in which the tip of the sword has been lowered from *chudan-no-kamae* to the opponent's kneecap.

hakama A pleated garment that covers the waist down to the ankles, divided into two sections like pants and worn over the *gi* (shirt); it is commonly blue (indigo), black, or white.

harai-waza A *waza* used when the opponent is in a defensive stance and there is no opportunity to attack; it consists of deflecting the opponent's *shinai* up to the left or right, or down to the left or right, and striking as one breaks down the opponent's stance.

hasso-no-kamae A stance where the left foot is half a step forward from the *chudan* stance and the right fist is raised so the *tsuba* is at the height of the mouth and the sword is pulled upright against the right shoulder; this stance is rarely used in today's kendo.

hidar Left; to the left.

hiki-waza A *waza* where one strikes while retreating in situations where one is very close to the opponent or after the opponent has become unguarded.

hiraki-ashi The footwork used when striking or defending with the body turned diagonally.

iaido A form of *kenjitsu* (art of the sword) that is performed with one or both knees on the ground and involves a quick draw of the sword to slash an opponent.

ippon shobu One-cut duel fought with real swords, once a life-or-death event.

ippon-uchi A way of striking where one first selects a striking zone, then makes the first strike naturally, powerfully, and with an accord of spirit, sword, and body (*ki-ken-tai*).

issoku-itto-no-maai A fighting distance of approximately 72 inches (180 cm) between oneself and the opponent; also called *issoku-ittoi*.

jodan-no-kamae One of the five stances in kendo where the *shinai* is held above the head; an offensive stance in which the *shinai* is held with both hands and either the right or left foot is forward.

kaeshi-do Blocking a strike with the side of the sword.

kaeshi-waza A type of *waza* used to respond to an opponent's striking move where one catches the opponent's *shinai* with his own *shinai*, parries, then immediately executes a counterstrike.

kake-go A natural vocalization that shows that one is full of spirit and on guard.

kamae A posture or stance; a state of readiness.

kamiza The position where one of seniority sits. In the dojo, the position of the altar or shrine.

kata A model or form that depicts in detail the ideal states of the mind, *waza*, and body that are acquired through practice.

katana A single-edged sword with a blade length of greater than twenty-five inches.

katsu To fight and defeat the opponent; to surpass.

keiko Practice, as opposed to contest.

ken A double-edged sword.

kendo A form of budo that aims to train the mind and body and to cultivate one's character through one-to-one striking practice using a bamboo or synthetic sword or *shinai* while wearing protective equipment or armor. The term *kendo* was developed in 1919 in Japan by the unifying organization for the martial arts at the time. The arts of fencing (gekken and *kenjitsu*) were renamed kendo, the way of the sword.

kendo-gi A kimono-style top that is suitable for kendo practices and matches; most have tight, short sleeves, are made of quilted cotton, and are navy, indigo, or white.

kendo-gu *See* bogu.

kensen The tip of the sword or *shinai*.

kiai The act of concentrating on one's opponent's moves and one's planned moves, and mounting a challenge with utmost caution; also the vocalization one produces when in an intense state of kendo mind.

kihon A foundation or basis.

kime A decision, ruling, or conclusion; concentrating on scoring a *waza*. Also refers to the way of gripping the *shinai* when striking.

kobudo In contrast to *budo*, which has become more sportslike, a type of martial art that has kept its ancient mode of training and has been preserved and handed down from generation to generation; also called *koryu*.

kodachi A short sword; in kendo, the wooden sword (*bokuto*) used in *kata*. It is the shorter of the two *bokuto* and is also called *shoto*.

koryu *See* kobudo.

kote The glove worn on each of the hands that covers the part of the arm from the tips of the fingers to the elbow; a type of *waza* in which one strikes the opponent's wrist.

maai The spatial distance between two opponents.

men The piece of kendo armor that covers the head, face, throat, and shoulders; a type of *waza* in which one strikes the top of the opponent's head.

metsuke Positioning of the eyes; a way of looking at an opponent in which one, always cautious of the tip of the opponent's sword, looks into the opponent's eyes while also paying attention to his entire body.

mittsu-no-sen The three *sen*. *Sensen-no-sen* is winning by forestalling the opponent's attack with one's own attack. *Senzen-no-sen* is winning by striking in turn before the opponent's strike is successful. *Go-no-sen* is winning by first striking down the opponent's sword or parrying, then attacking strongly when the opponent has become discouraged.

mokuso A courtesy performed with everyone sitting together in meditation at the beginning and end of *keiko*; the meditation is performed sitting in the *seiza* position, with the left hand on top of the right hand and the thumbs touching each other.

monouchi The part of the sword blade located about ten centimeters from the tip; in the case of the *shinai*, the part of the cutting edge where force is used most efficiently.

motodachi The one who takes on the role of the instructor in *keiko*.

musha-shugyo Pilgrimage; knight errantry; a training method with the aim of improving one's skills during one's travels from place to place.

nidan-waza A combination of techniques consisting of two consecutive strikes and thrusts made in a single continuous motion.

nuki-waza A type of *waza* in which one evades an attacking opponent, causing the opponent to swing through the air, then counterattacks when the opponent has stopped.

obi A long, narrow sash that is wrapped around the waist on top of a kimono or *kendo-gi*; also, that which is used to secure hip protectors or *hakama* to the body.

odachi The long sword; the longer of the two *bokuto*; also called the *daito*.

oji-waza A type of *waza* that involves stopping the attacking opponent's technique by manipulating one's body and sword (parrying) and then finding the opponent's weakness (*suki*) and counterattacking.

okuri-ashi The most basic footwork used in kendo; moving by stepping forward with the foot closest to the direction of movement, then immediately moving the other foot forward as if to send it into the first foot. Movement can be in any of the eight directions: forward, backward, to the left, to the right, or diagonally.

omote When facing an opponent, one's right side, or the corresponding left side of the opponent; the left face of one's own *shinai* when in the middle (*chudan*) position.

rei Formal bow.

ryu Martial arts tradition or school.

ryuha A branch or section of a traditional school.

sabaku To move to an advantageous position by manipulating one's body and *shinai*.

seiza Literally, correct (*sei*) seat (*za*); a way of sitting with both knees together and the shins and the top of the feet on the floor.

sen A state of mind in which one forestalls one's attacker by knowing the exact second he is going to cut and beginning one's own *waza* against him immediately before his attack.

sensei Teacher or instructor.

shiai Kendo contest or tournament.

shidachi During *kata* practice, the one in the position of the disciple or student; the person opposite the *uchidachi*.

shinai A sword modeled after the Japanese *katana*, made of either bamboo or synthetic materials and used in kendo practices and matches. It is made up of four split staves, the tip and handle are wrapped in leather, and it is fitted with a sword guard (*tsuba*).

shinken-shobu A seriously fought match.

shinogi The raised edge that runs from the end of the *tsuba* to the tip of the blade on either side and is located between the top of the blade and the blade's cutting edge.

shitate Inferiority; a position lower than others; a person of low rank.

shizentai A basic kendo posture that is stable, balanced, and natural and from which one can move one's body or respond to an opponent's moves quickly, accurately, and freely.

shomen The front face or center of the head; straight ahead; in places such as a kendo dojo, the place where the altar or shrine is located; also, the central section of the striking zone of the *men*.

shomen-uchi A strike to the center of the *men*.

sonkyu A ready position; squatting on the balls of one's feet, heels off the floor, buttocks lowered, knees opened outward, and the upper body upright.

suki The gap or space between two objects; also, loosening one's attention or dropping one's guard; a weakness; an opportunity that should be taken.

suriage The act of deflecting a striking opponent's *shinai* with one's own *shinai*, swinging it upward from below as if drawing an arc with the *kensen*.

suriage-waza A *waza* in which one deflects the striking opponent's *shinai* by swiping it upward with the right or the left of one's own sword and then strikes when the direction of the opponent's *shinai* or his balance has been upset.

suri-ashi The act of walking without lifting the feet, by dragging the bottom of the feet across the floor.

taiatari The act of colliding into the opponent with the strike's surplus of force.

toi-maai In interval that is farther than *issoku-itto-no-maai*; the best distance for defending oneself against the opponent's attack; also called *to-ma*.

tsuba A sword guard, or plate that is inserted between the hilt and the blade of the sword to protect the hand that grips the hilt.

tsuba-zeriai The situation in which the distance between oneself and the opponent is the closest, both players are holding their *shinai* tilted slightly to the right, and the sword guards (*tsuba*) or fists are locked against one another.

tsuburi A heavy dueling sword.

tsugi-ashi A basic type of footwork mainly used when striking from a long distance; the left (back) foot is pulled in close to the right foot, then the right foot immediately takes a big step forward.

tsuka The hilt of the sword; the handle of the *shinai*; the region of the sword or *shinai* that is gripped with both hands.

tsuki Thrust; one of the striking and thrusting zones in kendo; name of throat flap on men.

tsuki-waza General name for a *waza* where one thrusts at the opponent's throat zone.

uchi Strikes or cuts.

uchidachi During *kata* practice, the one in the position of instructor or leader; the person opposite the *shidachi*.

uchikomi Striking practice conducted alone or using a stand or stick held up by another.

uchikomi-bo A stick that is held up for another in striking practice in the stage before practicing with armor; practice with such a stick.

uchikome-dai A stand used in striking practice conducted alone; practice with such a stand.

uchikomi-ningyo A dummy used in striking practice conducted alone; practice with such a dummy.

uchi-ma The most effective distance (*maai*) from which to strike an opponent.

ura When facing an opponent, one's left side, or the corresponding right side of the opponent; the right face of one's own *shinai* when in the middle stance (*chudan*).

uwate Superiority; one whose abilities, skills, or scholastic achievements is superior to others.

waki-no-kamae The stance in which the right arm is pulled back from the *chudan* stance and the sword is held below the right armpit, with the tip of the sword pointing backward and the blade facing down.

waza A movement based on a standard form that is used to challenge and defeat the opponent.

zanshin The state of keeping alert and guarded after striking in case of a counterattack by the opponent.